THE ART OF SEQUENCING
A STEP BY STEP APPROACH

BY DON MURO

Editor: Joseph Muro
Computer Graphics (Text): Garry Simpson
Cover Design: Ann France

Copyright © 1993 CPP/Belwin, Inc.
15800 N.W. 48th Avenue, Miami FL 33014

TABLE OF CONTENTS

FOREWORD

New technologies often simplify or revolutionize existing job tasks. MIDI, synthesizers, and the sequencer represent such a technological revolution. The ability to hear a performance of a musical work as it is being composed opens new doors to both the accomplished musician as well as the student. The musician can focus on the important issues of music - the performance and the sound itself. Now, for the first time in history, a musician can sit at a music workstation and compose music, part by instrumental part, actually hearing the music as it is being written. At the end of this interactive process, the sequence may be used as the final product and released as a recorded work, or transferred to standard music notation for further performance by instrumentalists.

These powerful tools represent a fundamental change in work habits. New skills must be learned to take full advantage of these new tools. This book presents a musical and simplified approach to learning how to use the sequencer. Don Muro is an accomplished musician, technologist, and most importantly, an excellent teacher. The combination of these skills is rare and thus makes the author uniquely qualified to address the process of learning these technologies.

The Art of Sequencing presents a thorough approach to sequencing regardless of whether you are using a hardware or software-based sequencer, or even using an integrated workstation instrument. By integrating the realization of music into the step by step learning process, Don Muro turns your focus away from button-pressing and towards the real issues of making music.

Sequencers can change the way you create music. This book can help you take control and get the most out of this exciting musical revolution.

David S. Mash
Assistant Dean of Curriculum
for Academic Technology
Berklee College of Music
Boston, Massachusetts

INTRODUCTION

This book was written for musicians who want to learn the art of sequencing in the simplest and most direct way. With this goal in mind, I have attempted to do the following:
- To teach and to reinforce the basic techniques of sequencing.
- To present the material in a series of easy-to-follow sequential steps.
- To define technical terms within the text itself.
- To eliminate all extraneous material that might interfere with a hands-on approach.

In order to achieve these goals, I have organized the book so that each chapter is a self-contained, step by step lesson that will enable you to master a specific technique. Each lesson has a beginning, a middle and an end. Many lessons share common beginning steps that may seem needlessly repetitious. However, the repetition is deliberate; it serves as review and reinforcement. Repetition also precludes the necessity of referring to previous chapters for common beginning steps in a lesson. Because the chapters are treated as self-contained units, they can easily be adapted for a wide variety of teaching and learning situations.

It is my hope that this book will help you to understand basic sequencing techniques and will guide you in creating musical sequences of your own.

ACKNOWLEDGMENTS

There are many people I would like to thank for their help in the preparation of this book. Space limitations prevent me from listing the hundreds of music educators who participated in my summer workshops and who graciously field-tested preliminary versions of this book. I would be remiss, however, if I did not thank D. Larry Bachtell for proofreading an early version of the book, and for offering many valuable suggestions. Thanks are also due to David Mash for additional suggestions and for taking the time to write the foreword. I also want to thank Mercer Stockell for his willingness to share his vast knowledge of technical information and Garry Simpson for his help with the graphics and with the layout.

The production of this book would not have been possible without the help of three people. I want to thank my wife, Deanna, for her computer assistance, and Sandy Feldstein for his editorial advice and his patience. Finally, I want to thank my father, Joseph Muro. Without his support, vision, direction, and editorial skills, this book would never have been written.

ABOUT THE BOOK

The Art of Sequencing is divided into three sections that deal with MIDI concepts, recording techniques and editing techniques.

- Section 1 (**Concepts and Terminology**) covers essential background information that you will need before you begin the hands-on portion of the book.

- Section 2 (**Recording Techniques**) deals with the skills and techniques needed to create sequences. In writing this book, I have tried to accommodate all makes and types of synthesizers and sequencers. As a result, I have included some material that may not apply to you. For example, if you are using a multi-timbral synthesizer, you will skip Chapter 6. If you are using a mono-timbral synthesizer, you will skip Chapter 5. Whenever the material does not apply to your equipment, it will be clearly indicated.

- Section 3 (**Basic Editing Techniques**) deals with specific techniques for correcting and improving your sequences.

Although the chapters in the book are organized sequentially, it is possible to change the order to achieve your personal goals. For example, you might choose to learn how to correct wrong notes (Chapter 7) after you have recorded a single-track sequence (Chapter 3).

Some readers may notice the absence of step recording - a process of entering notes by typing note names on a keypad or by holding keys on a keyboard and then entering information about the loudness and the duration of each note. I have omitted a discussion of step recording for two reasons. First, the wide variation in step recording techniques would make it extremely difficult to create a generic step by step approach that would work with every sequencer. Second, step recording frequently results in music that sounds mechanical and inexpressive. In most cases, readers with minimal keyboard skills can create musical sequences more easily by recording parts at a slow tempo and by using the editing techniques described in Section 3 of this book.

Classroom teachers can increase the effectiveness of this book by preparing a user's guide for the actual instruments and equipment that the students will be using. The guide should include specific information from owners' manuals that might be helpful in implementing the techniques discussed in this book.

Feel free to substitute different music for the sequencing techniques in Section 2. I chose to use the same musical excerpt throughout the section to make it easier to concentrate on mastering sequencing techniques instead of learning new music.

SECTION 1

CONCEPTS AND TERMINOLOGY

In Section 1, you will learn the basic concepts of MIDI. You will also learn the basic concepts of sequencing. An understanding of these concepts will help you to create music using any MIDI synthesizer and any sequencer.

Chapter 1

AN OVERVIEW OF MIDI

Before we can discuss sequencing techniques, you must first have a basic understanding of MIDI. Every sequencer available today uses MIDI to communicate with electronic instruments and equipment. In this chapter, I will not attempt to explain all of the technical aspects of MIDI. Instead, I will focus on the concepts that are directly related to sequencers and sequencing techniques. These concepts can be explained by answering the four questions most often asked about MIDI.

WHAT IS MIDI?

MIDI stands for the Musical Instrument Digital Interface. The phrase "Musical Instrument" is self explanatory. **Digital** means dealing with numbers. In MIDI applications, the numbers are actually a series of voltages that represent two digits - "0" and "1". The word **interface** in this context can be defined as a connection that allows two or more devices to communicate. Therefore, the acronym MIDI can be defined as a communication system that enables MIDI-equipped instruments and computers to send and to receive digital information.

HOW WAS MIDI DEVELOPED?

The MIDI concept was originally developed by a small group of synthesizer manufacturers in 1981. These manufacturers saw the need to standardize instruments and equipment so that the industry as a whole could improve and expand. As a result, they developed an interface design that has become the accepted standard for the industry. By the end of 1982, most synthesizer manufacturers were preparing to incorporate MIDI into their new product designs. The unofficial debut of MIDI took place at the National Association of Music Merchandisers (NAMM) show in January of 1983. A synthesizer made in Japan was connected by a MIDI cable to a synthesizer made in America. This connection made it possible to play both instruments from one keyboard. The ramifications of this first experiment proved to be monumental. MIDI is affecting almost every aspect of the music world in ways that were previously unimaginable.

WHAT KIND OF INFORMATION IS TRANSMITTED AND RECEIVED THROUGH MIDI?

The information that is transmitted and received through a MIDI communication system will be described in detail in Chapter 2. At this point, however, it is important to understand a few basic concepts. MIDI cables cannot transmit audio signals. Audio signals cannot travel through MIDI cables. MIDI cables can, however, transmit **musical performance information** in much the same way that a player piano records information about a performance on a piano. The piano roll does not produce sound by itself; we still need the piano to hear the performance. The piano roll contains information about the performance - what keys were played, when the keys were played, how hard the keys were struck, and when foot pedals were used. MIDI performances operate in much the same manner. MIDI converts the physical aspects of your performance into digital information that can be sent to other MIDI instruments.

HOW DOES MIDI WORK?

In simple terms, MIDI is similar to a telephone system. If a telephone has a standard telephone plug, it can be connected to any standard telephone receptacle. It can then communicate with any other telephone by sending and by receiving messages. MIDI equipped instruments work in much the same way; however, they require a special coupling cable with a five pin plug on both ends. These cables are like telephone lines; they link the system and carry information from one source to another. Telephones are most often used to carry verbal information to and from any other telephone in the system. They can accomplish this because telephones have a mouthpiece for talking (a transmitter), and an ear piece for listening (a receiver).

Most MIDI-equipped instruments also use devices that function as transmitters and receivers to generate and to receive MIDI data. The MIDI IN port on a MIDI-equipped instrument functions as a receiver; it accepts incoming information that is generated by an external source - for example, by another synthesizer. The MIDI OUT port functions as a transmitter; it sends out information that is generated internally. Let's look and see how these connectors work.

MIDI IN and MIDI OUT

MIDI makes it possible to connect two or more synthesizers so that when the keyboard of one synthesizer is played, the other synthesizer responds as if its keyboard is also being played. Pipe organs and harpsichords with at least two keyboards can produce the same effect by using devices called couplers. The individual sounds of each keyboard on an organ or on a harpsichord can be coupled to one **master** keyboard, making it possible to produce an ensemble sound of considerable complexity. The master keyboard is always the keyboard that is played manually, while the **slave** keyboard is controlled by the coupler mechanism. MIDI-equipped instruments can achieve similar coupling effects simply by using MIDI cables. *Fig. 1.1* represents the most basic type of MIDI connection - two synthesizers connected by one MIDI cable. In this example Synthesizer A is the master synthesizer, and Synthesizer B is the slave synthesizer.

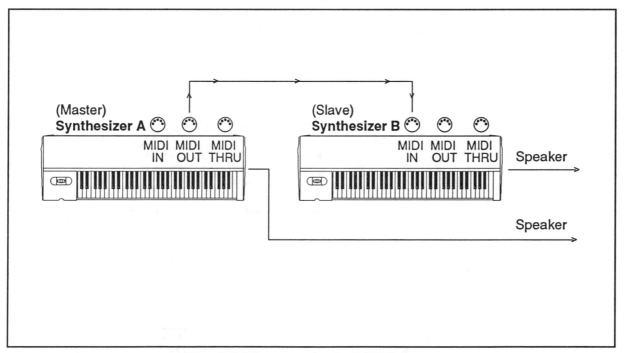

Fig. 1.1 The most basic MIDI setup.

In *Fig. 1.1* we have two synthesizers that we want to play simultaneously from one keyboard. We'll label them Synthesizer A and Synthesizer B. If you want both synthesizers to produce sound when you play the keyboard of Synthesizer A, then Synthesizer A will be considered your master keyboard, and Synthesizer B will be your slave keyboard. When you play Synthesizer A, the MIDI cable will carry the performance information from the MIDI OUT port on Synthesizer A to the MIDI IN port on Synthesizer B. The **MIDI O U T** port is a **transmitter**; it sends out information that is generated internally. The **MIDI IN** port is a **receiver**; it accepts incoming information that is generated by an external source.

For example, if you play the low C on Synthesizer A's keyboard, you will hear the sound of Synthesizer A, and, at the same time, the sound of the low C on Synthesizer B. The command to "play low C" is transmitted from the MIDI OUT port of Synthesizer A to the MIDI IN port of Synthesizer B. When the circuitry in Synthesizer B receives this command, it will play the low C sound exactly the way Synthesizer A plays it. Because the command from Synthesizer A to Synthesizer B is transmitted internally, you will not see any physical activity on the keyboard of Synthesizer B. See *Fig. 1.2*.

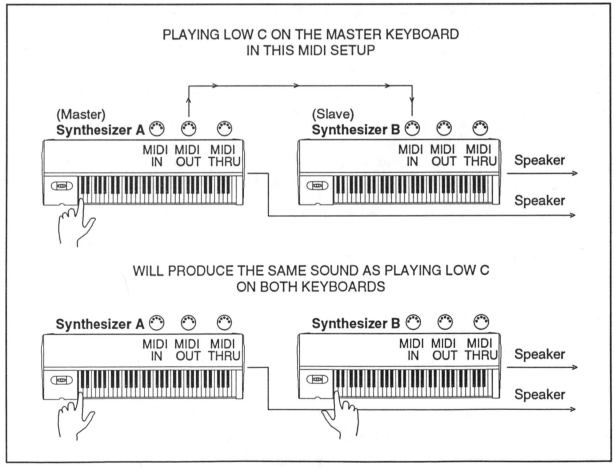

Fig. 1.2

MIDI THRU

So far you have learned the functions of two ports - MIDI IN and MIDI OUT. The third and last MIDI connector is called the MIDI **THRU** port. The MIDI THRU port functions as a **relayer**. It receives a copy of the information that is sent to the MIDI IN port, and relays the information to another instrument. Look at *Fig. 1.3* to see how the MIDI THRU port can be used.

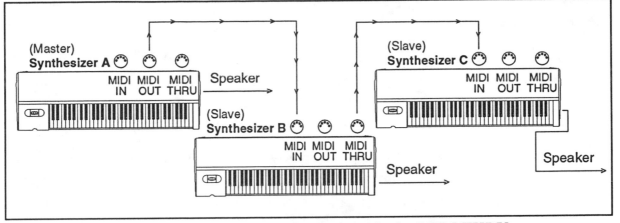

Fig. 1.3 Connecting three synthesizers with the MIDI THRU port.

In *Fig. 1.3* three synthesizers are connected so that all three instruments can be played from one keyboard. Synthesizer A (the master keyboard) can transmit MIDI data to Synthesizers B and C (the slaves). If you play Synthesizer A's keyboard, the MIDI cable will carry the information from the MIDI OUT port on Synthesizer A to the MIDI IN port on Synthesizer B. This connection will enable Synthesizer B to play simultaneously any notes that you play on Synthesizer A. Notice that you have a second MIDI cable connecting Synthesizer B with Synthesizer C. In this connection, you use the MIDI THRU port of Synthesizer B to relay information from Synthesizer A to Synthesizer C. Now when you play Synthesizer A you will hear Synthesizer B **and** Synthesizer C.

If you understand what has been discussed so far, you should be able to answer the following question: Using the setup in *Fig. 1.3*, what instruments, if any, would sound if you played Synthesizer B? Here are some possible answers:

1. You would hear all three synthesizers.

2. You would hear nothing.

3. You would hear Synthesizers B and C.

4. You would hear only Synthesizer B.

Take a moment to think through the problem yourself before you read the following answers.

• **Answer #1**, "You would hear all three synthesizers," is wrong. In this setup Synthesizer A can only **send** information. Synthesizer A's MIDI IN port is not connected to receive information; therefore, Synthesizer A will produce sound only when its keyboard is played.

• **Answer #2**, "You would hear nothing," is also wrong. All three instruments are connected to speakers. Since you are playing Synthesizer B's keyboard, you must, at the very least, hear the sound of Synthesizer B.

• **Answer #3**, "You would hear Synthesizers B and C," is also wrong. At first glance, you might think that answer #3 is correct since a MIDI cable from Synthesizer B is connected to Synthesizer C's MIDI IN port. The cable, however, is connected to Synthesizer B's MIDI THRU port. Remember, the MIDI THRU port merely relays information from one external source to another; in this setup, Synthesizer B's MIDI THRU port is ready to relay information from Synthesizer A to Synthesizer C. Since you are not playing Synthesizer A's keyboard, however, Synthesizer C will not produce any sound.

• **Answer #4**, "You would hear only Synthesizer B," is the correct answer.

So far you have learned that if you play Synthesizer A in *Fig. 1.3*, you will hear the sounds of all three instruments. If you play Synthesizer B, you will hear only the sound of Synthesizer B. What would happen if you played Synthesizer C? Again, take a moment and see if you can think of the correct answer.

If you played Synthesizer C, only Synthesizer C would produce sound. Since the MIDI OUT port on Synthesizer C is not being used, neither of the other synthesizers will receive any information; therefore, they will not produce any sound.

Before we go any further, let's take a moment to review the functions of the three types of MIDI connector ports:

• **MIDI IN** is a **receiver**; it receives MIDI data from an external source.
• **MIDI OUT** is a **transmitter**; it sends MIDI data that is generated internally.
• **MIDI THRU** is a **relayer**; it relays MIDI data from an external source to another MIDI instrument.

It might also be helpful to remember that there are only five different ways to connect instruments in a MIDI setup. Here are the choices:

1. When only the MIDI OUT port of an instrument is connected, that instrument can function only as a master. It transmits MIDI data, but it cannot receive or relay data.

2. When only the MIDI IN port of an instrument is connected, that instrument can function only as a slave. It can receive MIDI data, but it cannot send or relay data.

3. When both the MIDI IN and the MIDI THRU ports are connected, an instrument can function either as a slave, or as a relayer of MIDI data to other slaves. It can also function simultaneously as a slave and a relayer.

4. When both the MIDI IN and the MIDI OUT ports are connected, an instrument can function as a master controller or as a slave. It can also function simultaneously as a master and a slave. In other words, it can send data to control other instruments through its MIDI OUT port, and at the same time, it can be controlled by external MIDI data coming into its MIDI IN port.

5. When the MIDI IN, MIDI OUT, and MIDI THRU ports are all connected, an instrument can function as a master, as a slave, or as a relayer. It can also function simultaneously as a master and a slave, as a master and a relayer, as a slave and a relayer, or as a master, a slave, and a relayer. In other words, it can send data to control other instruments through its MIDI OUT port, and at the same time, it can be controlled by external MIDI data coming into its MIDI IN port. It can also relay this external MIDI data to other slaves through its MIDI THRU port. (See *Fig. 1.4*)

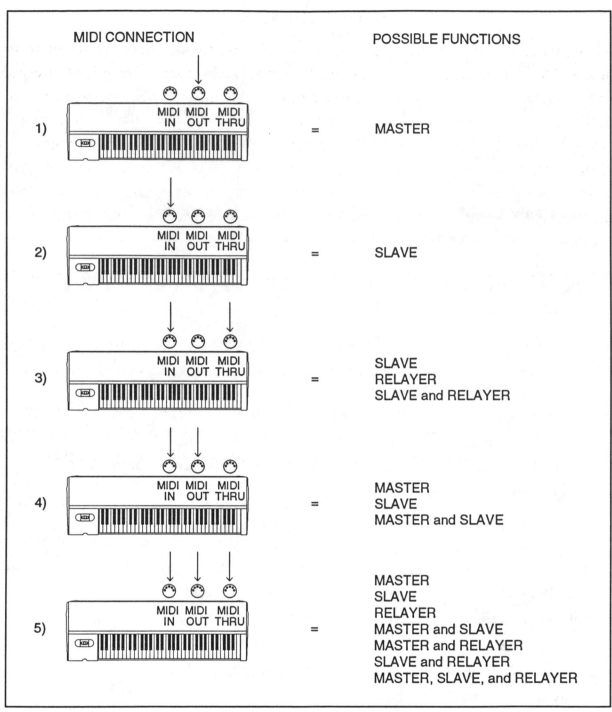

Fig. 1.4 The five types of MIDI connections.

The five connections displayed in *Fig. 1.4* are the only ways that an instrument can be used in a MIDI setup. It's important for you to understand these connections, because the vast majority of MIDI setup problems deal with improperly connected MIDI cables, and with a misunderstanding of MIDI channels.

MIDI CHANNELS

MIDI data can be transmitted and received on 16 separate channels numbered from 1 through 16. All channels function identically - that is, no channel has priority over any other channel. MIDI channels are similar to TV channels. When you want to see a particular TV program, you merely set the TV controller on the desired channel number. Your TV set will receive the program while ignoring all other programs on all other channels. MIDI channels work in a similar way. When you want one MIDI equipped instrument to communicate with other MIDI instruments, you must set all instruments to the same channel number. If you fail to do this, no communication will take place.

For example, even though a radio receives dozens of broadcast frequencies at once, it can tune in or play only one frequency (or station) at a time. If the broadcast frequency of your favorite FM radio station is 95.5, your radio must be set to 95.5 in order for you to hear a broadcast. In other words, the radio (**receiver**) must be set to the same frequency (**channel**) as the broadcast frequency of the radio station (**transmitter**).

In *Fig. 1.5*, Synthesizer A is transmitting MIDI data on Channel 1. Synthesizer B, however, is set to receive and execute MIDI data on Channel 2. Even though Synthesizer A's MIDI data is received by the MIDI IN port on Synthesizer B, Synthesizer B ignores the data because it is sent on the wrong channel. If you play low C on Synthesizer A you will hear only the sound of Synthesizer A. The MIDI connection will not work, even though the MIDI cable is properly connected. The instruments are trying to communicate on two different channels. This cannot be done.

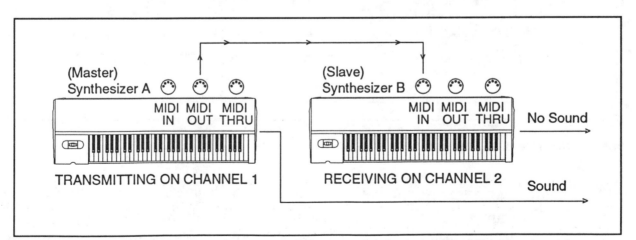

Fig. 1.5 In this example, you will hear only the sound of Synthesizer A.

The MIDI communication problem in *Fig. 1.5* can be solved in two ways. Remember, in order for the MIDI data to be executed, Synthesizer A and Synthesizer B must communicate on the same channel. You can accomplish this either by changing Synthesizer A's MIDI transmitting channel from Channel 1 to Channel 2, or by changing Synthesizer B's MIDI receiving channel from Channel 2 to Channel 1. Remember, it makes no difference which channel you use as long as both instruments are communicating on the same channel. See *Fig. 1.6*.

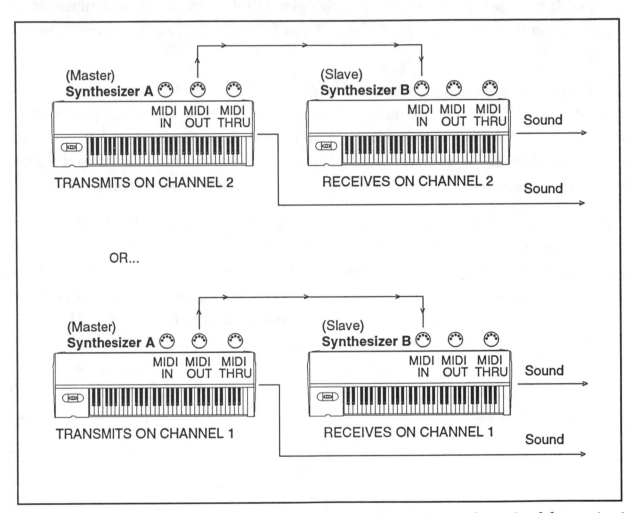

Fig. 1.6 The communication problem shown in Fig. 1.5 can be solved by assigning both synthesizers to the same MIDI channel.

At this point, you may be wondering why you need 16 channels. This question will be answered in Chapter 5. For now, remember that in all MIDI setups, the cable connections between instruments must be correct and the channel numbers must match.

Chapter 2

AN OVERVIEW OF SEQUENCERS

In Chapter 1, you learned about the basics of MIDI. In this chapter, you will focus on sequencers and on the basic concepts of sequencing. This material can be covered by answering the five questions most often asked about sequencers and sequencing.

WHAT IS A SEQUENCER?

A sequencer is a device that **records** and plays back performance information. Sequencers also make it possible to change or to **edit** almost any aspect of this performance information. For example, most sequencers will allow you to correct wrong notes, to change tempo, to play back a song in a different key, and to change instrumental sounds. A sequencer also makes it possible to save or to **store** performance information, usually on a computer disk. This storage capability will allow you to retrieve the data and **play back** any song at a later time without having to re-record the music. A sequencer, therefore, is a device that can **record**, **edit**, **store**, and **play back** digital data that represents a musical performance. Remember, sequencers do not record sound.

ARE ALL SEQUENCERS ALIKE?

There are three types of sequencers - **hardware** sequencers, **software** sequencers, and **integrated** sequencers. A **hardware** sequencer is a separate, stand alone component. Although most hardware sequencers have no internal sound generating capabilities, they include features such as built-in MIDI ports and, usually, an internal disk drive for storing data.

Software sequencers are computer programs that enable a computer to function as a sequencer. The term **software** can be defined as digital data that instructs a computer or other hardware how to perform a particular function. Software sequencers usually consist of at least one floppy disk and an owner's manual. At the present time, most computers are not manufactured with built-in MIDI ports. Therefore, most software sequencers require the use of a MIDI **computer interface**. In Chapter 1, we defined the term **interface** as a connection that allows two or more instruments or devices to communicate with each other. A MIDI computer interface, then, is a device that allows synthesizers and other MIDI equipped instruments to communicate with a computer. A MIDI computer interface is usually an add-on component which takes the form of a small circuit board about the size of a 3"x 5" card. *Fig. 2.1* shows the most basic connection of one synthesizer, a MIDI computer interface, and a computer.

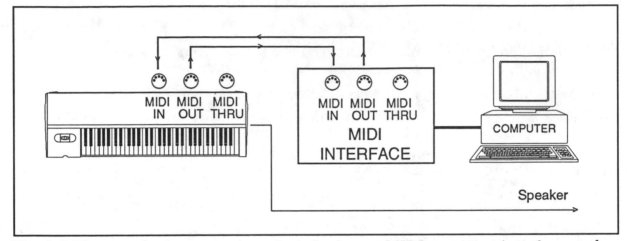

Fig. 2.1 The most basic connection of synthesizer, a MIDI computer interface, and a computer. (On most computers, the MIDI interface is installed inside the computer.)

Integrated sequencers are sequencers built into most electronic musical instruments such as synthesizers or drum machines. Most of today's electronic instruments contain integrated sequencers; some are more powerful than others.

WHAT TYPES OF DATA DOES A SEQUENCER RECORD AND PLAY BACK?

In Chapter 1, you learned that MIDI devices transmit information about musical performances. You also learned that the digital data traveling through MIDI cables represents messages or commands that are expressed by a series of zeros and ones. These zeros and ones can represent many different types of information, depending upon the specific instruments and devices used in a MIDI setup. This book will focus on MIDI **channel voice messages** - the type of information most useful for sequencing. MIDI channel voice messages can include the following information:

- **Note-On** - this message signals the beginning of a note. Whenever you press a key on the keyboard, a note-on message sends out a "Start playing NOW!" command. The note-on message also includes information indicating how quickly a key is struck. This information is called either the attack velocity level or simply the velocity level. The velocity level is often used to control the loudness and brightness of a note.

- **Note-Off** - this message signals the end of a note. Whenever you release a key on the keyboard, a note-off message sends out a "Stop playing NOW!" command. On some instruments, the note-off message also includes information indicating how quickly a key has been released. This information is called the release velocity level.

- **Program Change** - the word **program** is used to describe a preset sound in an instrument's memory. A preset sound contains specific information about pitch, loudness, tone quality, and other properties of sound. For example, Program 1 might be a piano sound, Program 2 might be a guitar sound, and so on. A program change message signals a program change on your instrument. For example, when you push a button to select Program 3 on your instrument, a program change message sends out a "Go to Program 3 NOW!" command.

- **Pitch Bend** - the pitch bend change message sends information about the pitch bend controller. Whenever you move the pitch bender on your instrument, the pitch bend change message sends out a stream of digital information that represents the physical movement of the pitch bender.

- **Aftertouch** (sometimes called **pressure sensitivity**) - aftertouch information is generated on many electronic keyboards by applying additional pressure to a key after it is depressed. As the key is pressed harder and harder, more and more information is transmitted. This information is commonly used to increase the brightness of a sound or to increase the amount of vibrato.

- **Control Change** - the control change message sends information about a setting for a controller. Controllers include devices such as volume pedals and sustain switches.

Note on, note off, program change, pitch bend, aftertouch, and **control change** - these are the messages that you will be working with in this book. The ways in which these messages are generated, recorded, and edited will determine the musicality of your sequences.

> *Note: Not all MIDI equipped instruments can transmit or receive all of these messages. For example, most MIDI equipped digital pianos do not use pitch bend controllers or generate aftertouch data. Most MIDI equipped drum machines do not transmit program change commands. The more messages that an instrument can transmit and receive, the greater the expressive capabilities of the instrument.*

HOW DOES A SEQUENCER WORK?

We have already defined a sequencer as a device that is capable of recording, editing, storing, and playing back digital data that represents a musical performance. To better understand this definition, look at *Fig. 2.2*.

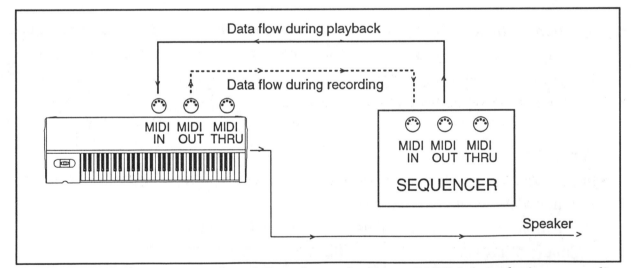

Fig. 2.2 In this diagram the dotted line shows the flow of MIDI data during recording. The solid line shows the MIDI data flow during playback.

In *Fig. 2.2*, one MIDI cable connects the MIDI OUT port of the synthesizer to the MIDI IN port on the sequencer. This connection enables the sequencer to record MIDI data generated by the synthesizer. The second MIDI cable connects the MIDI OUT port of the sequencer to the MIDI IN port on the synthesizer. This connection enables the synthesizer to produce sound when it receives the MIDI data played back from the sequencer.

Let's examine the recording and playback functions in greater detail.

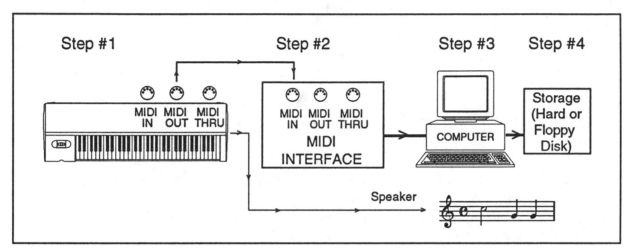

Fig. 2.3 A closer look at the MIDI data flow during the recording process.

Here's what happens in *Fig. 2.3*:

- **Step 1** - The music performed on the keyboard is converted to MIDI data by the MIDI processor inside the synthesizer. In other words, the MIDI processor converts every aspect of the performance into digital data.

- **Step 2** - The MIDI data from the synthesizer travels through a MIDI cable into the MIDI computer interface.

- **Step 3** - The computer interface sends data into the computer memory.

- **Step 4** - The data is stored permanently on a hard disk or a floppy disk.

In *Fig. 2.4* you will see how the sequencer plays back the musical performance.

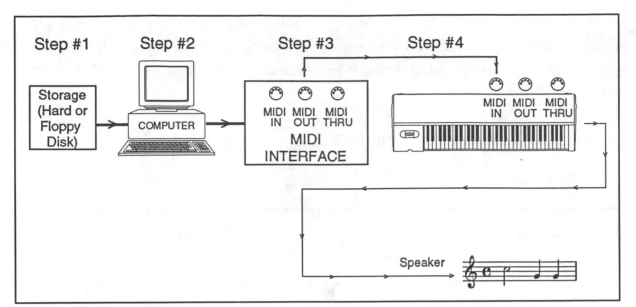

Fig. 2.4 A closer look at the MIDI data flow during playback.

- **Step 1** - The data stored on a hard disk or a floppy disk is loaded into the computer memory.
- **Step 2** - The computer reads the data and sends the data out to the MIDI computer interface.
- **Step 3** - The data travels through the computer interface and into the MIDI IN port of the synthesizer.
- **Step 4** - The MIDI processor inside the synthesizer executes the performance information and the synthesizer reproduces the original performance.

WHAT ARE SEQUENCER TRACKS?

A sequencer track is a portion of computer memory assigned to record and play back MIDI data that represents a musical part such as a bass line, a piano part, or any instrumental part. For example, on Track 1 of the sequencer, you might record a synthesizer electric piano part. On Track 2, you might record a synthesizer bass part. On Track 3, you might record an electronic drum part. Some older sequencers have as few as two tracks, while other sequencers have dozens of tracks. Today, most sequencers offer at least eight tracks. The multi-track capability of sequencers makes it possible to build multi-layered musical arrangements by recording individual musical parts one at a time. This recording technique is called **overdubbing**. In Section 2, you will learn how to use MIDI overdubbing to create complete musical arrangements.

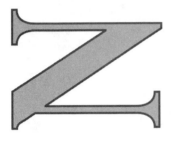
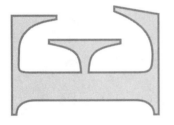

SECTION 2

RECORDING TECHNIQUES

In Section 1 of this book, you learned the basic concepts of MIDI and sequencers. In Secton 2, you will learn how to create single track sequences, multi-track sequences and multi-track and multi-timbral recording techniques you will be able to create complete electronic arrangements and orchestrations of your music.

Chapter 3

HOW TO CREATE A SINGLE-TRACK SEQUENCE

In Chapter 2, you learned about the types of sequencers. You also learned about sequencer tracks. In this chapter, you will learn how to create a sequence using one track. You will also learn how to use the playback features that are found on most sequencers.

In order to record your music as accurately as possible, you must set up the sequencer by selecting the time signature, the desired sound, and so on. The following procedure will work with almost every sequencer. If you are unsure of how to perform a particular function, check the owner's manual of the sequencer.

> *Note: In the following pages, the term "external sequencer" refers to hardware and software sequencers that are connected to the synthesizer with MIDI cables. The term "integrated sequencer" refers to sequencers that are built into an instrument.*

To record a sequence using one track, follow the steps below. In Part 1, you will learn how to create a setup chart that will serve as your master plan before you begin to record. In Part 2, you will learn how to use the information in the setup chart to record a single-track sequence.

PART 1 - CREATING A SETUP CHART

Step 1: Decide what you want to record.
You can record any kind of music using any sounds that you like. For this lesson, however, let's assume that you want to record the music in *Fig. 3.1*.

Fig. 3.1

Step 2: Make a setup chart to list the information that you will need when you begin to record the sequence.

In *Fig. 3.2*, you will see a partially completed setup chart that will help you to keep track of the information needed to create a sequence. In the first column, you should identify the contents (the musical part) that you plan to put on a specific sequencer track. For this lesson, assume that you identify the contents of the sequencer track by naming it "Melody". See *Fig. 3.2*. The remaining columns will be completed as you continue through the steps.

SETUP CHART

| | For External Sequencers | | | | |
Sequencer Track Name	Synthesizer MIDI Channel	Synthesizer Program Name	Synthesizer Program Number	Sequencer Track Number	Sequencer Track MIDI Channel
Melody					

Fig. 3.2

Step 3: If you are using an external sequencer, select and reserve a MIDI channel on the synthesizer to be used for the sequence.

Note: If you are using an integrated sequencer, skip this step.

You can use any MIDI channel, but for this lesson reserve MIDI Channel 5 on the synthesizer. Put this information in the setup chart. See *Fig. 3.3*.

SETUP CHART

| | For External Sequencers | | | | |
Sequencer Track Name	Synthesizer MIDI Channel	Synthesizer Program Name	Synthesizer Program Number	Sequencer Track Number	Sequencer Track MIDI Channel
Melody	5				

Fig. 3.3

Step 4: Select and reserve a program number on the synthesizer.

Suppose that you want to hear the music played with a piano sound, and suppose that the program number for the piano sound is 23. Reserve Program 23 on the synthesizer. See *Fig. 3.4*.

SETUP CHART

	For External Sequencers				
Sequencer Track Name	Synthesizer MIDI Channel	Synthesizer Program Name	Synthesizer Program Number	Sequencer Track Number	Sequencer Track MIDI Channel
Melody	5	Piano	23		

Fig. 3.4

Step 5: Select and reserve a sequencer track number for the instrumental part.

You can select any track. For this lesson, select Track 1. See *Fig. 3.5*.

SETUP CHART

	For External Sequencers				
Sequencer Track Name	Synthesizer MIDI Channel	Synthesizer Program Name	Synthesizer Program Number	Sequencer Track Number	Sequencer Track MIDI Channel
Melody	5	Piano	23	1	

Fig. 3.5

Step 6: Reserve the appropriate MIDI channel for the sequencer track.

If you are using an external sequencer, you already reserved MIDI Channel 5 for the synthesizer. (See Step 3.) Now reserve Channel 5 for Track 1 on the sequencer. (When recording with an external sequencer, remember that synthesizer MIDI channel numbers and sequencer track channel numbers should match.) If you are using an integrated sequencer, reserve Channel 5 for Track 1. See *Fig. 3.6*.

SETUP CHART

	For External Sequencers				
Sequencer Track Name	Synthesizer MIDI Channel	Synthesizer Program Name	Synthesizer Program Number	Sequencer Track Number	Sequencer Track MIDI Channel
Melody	5	Piano	23	1	5

Fig. 3.6

Now the setup chart is complete. Refer to it whenever necessary. For your convenience, you will find a duplicate setup chart (*Fig.3.6*) on p.153 which you may remove and use for reference when you record the melody.

PART 2 - RECORDING A SINGLE-TRACK SEQUENCE

Step 1: Make sure that the synthesizer and sequencer are turned on.
When you play the synthesizer, you should be able to hear its sound either through speakers or through headphones. If you are using an external sequencer, make sure that it is on.

Step 2: If you are using an external sequencer, set up the MIDI connections between the sequencer and the synthesizer.

Note: If you are using an integrated sequencer, skip this step.

Use one MIDI cable to connect the MIDI OUT port of the synthesizer to the MIDI IN port of the sequencer. Use another MIDI cable to connect the MIDI OUT port of the sequencer to the MIDI IN port of the synthesizer. Your MIDI connections should look like the connections shown in *Fig. 3.7*.

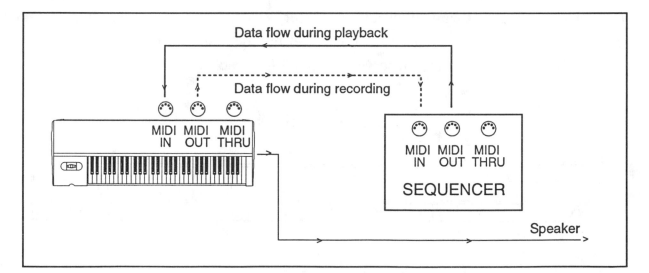

Fig. 3.7 The proper MIDI connections between a synthesizer and an external sequencer.

34

Step 3: If you are using an integrated sequencer, enter the sequencer mode.

> *Note: If you are using an external sequencer, skip this step.*

On most instruments, you can enter the sequencer mode by pressing a button labeled "SEQ" or "SEQUENCER". Consult your owner's manual to learn how to enter the sequencer mode of your instrument.

Step 4: Set the song tempo.

Suppose that you want to record the music in *Fig. 3.1* at a tempo of 80 *bpm (beats per minute)*. Set your song tempo indicator to this value. If you can't play the music at the indicated tempo, choose a slower tempo for the recording process. Be sure to change the tempo to the original value when you have finished recording. For example, if you feel more comfortable playing the melody at a metronome marking of 50 *bpm*, set the tempo indicator to 50 *bpm* and record the melody at this tempo. After you finish recording, change the tempo indicator to 80 *bpm,* and the sequencer will play back at the correct tempo.

Step 5: Set the time signature.

On most sequencers, you can enter the time signature by first locating the time signature on the sequencer screen and then entering the desired time signature. In this exercise, you would type "4" twice.

Step 6: Set the note (or record) resolution value to the highest resolution.

You will learn about sequencer resolution in Chapter 8. For now, set the resolution value to the highest resolution. The highest resolution will give you the most accurate playback of your performance.

Step 7: Activate the metronome.

It is not necessary to use the metronome when you are recording a sequence using only one track. However, since you will usually need to use a metronome when you record multi-track sequences, you should get used to recording with a metronome. If your sequencer allows you to specify the number of clicks per measure, adjust the metronome so that it clicks on every eighth note. Be sure that your synthesizer sound is soft enough for you to be able to hear the clicks.

Step 8: Set the number of lead-in measures for the metronome.
A **lead-in measure** allows you to hear one measure of metronome clicks before the sequencer begins recording. On some sequencers, it is possible to vary the number of lead-in measures. A one measure lead-in should work for this sequence.

Step 9: If you are using an external sequencer, assign the MIDI Channel number on the synthesizer to the appropriate channel number.

Note: If you are using an integrated sequencer, skip this step.

In the setup chart (*Fig.3.6*), you reserved Channel 5 for the synthesizer. The MIDI channel setting on most synthesizers is usually found in the "UTILITIES", "GLOBAL", or "MIDI" section of the instrument. (Consult your owner's manual to learn how to change the MIDI channel.)

Step 10: Assign Sequencer Track 1 to the appropriate MIDI channel.
In the setup chart (*Fig.3.6*), you reserved MIDI Channel 5 for Track 1 of the sequencer. Place the sequencer **cursor** on the line that designates the MIDI channel for Track 1 and set the channel number to 5. (The cursor is a blinking line or box on the sequencer screen.)

Step 11: If you are using an external sequencer, turn off the "MIDI ECHO" or "MIDI THRU" function on the sequencer.

Note: If you are using an integrated sequencer, skip this step.

If MIDI THRU is activated, the sequencer will send any incoming MIDI data through the sequencer's MIDI OUT port. When you play a note on the keyboard, the synthesizer will play two identical notes. The synthesizer's microprocessor (or "brain") receives one command to play a note from the keyboard and another command from the sequencer to play the same note. This doubling of every note changes the tone quality of certain sounds. It also reduces the number of notes that can be played simultaneously.

Step 12: Assign the sound for Track 1 on the sequencer.
In the setup chart (*Fig.3.6*), you selected the piano sound (Program 23). Place the sequencer cursor on the program number line for Track 1 and enter the number 23. (Be sure that Program 23 is selected on the synthesizer.)

Step 13: Identify the contents of Track 1 with a name.

If your sequencer allows you to name an empty track, place the cursor on the name line for Track 1 and type the word "Melody".

Step 14: Identify the sequence with a name.

If your sequencer allows you to name a song, place the cursor on the song title line and type the name "Fortress". Your sequencer screen should now look something like *Fig. 3.8*.

SONG NAME: Fortress			TIME SIG: 4/4
SONG TEMPO: 80	MIDI ECHO: Off		METRONOME: On

TRACK	NAME	MIDI CHANNEL	PROGRAM
1	Melody	5	23
2	_____	-	-
3	_____	-	-
4	_____	-	-
5	_____	-	-
6	_____	-	-
7	_____	-	-
8	_____	-	-

Fig. 3.8

Step 15: Record the sequence.

Now you are ready to record the sequence. On most sequencers, you begin recording by pressing a button labeled "RECORD", "REC", or "START". While you are recording, you will hear the sound of the metronome from the sequencer. The metronome will not be recorded.

TROUBLESHOOTING THE SEQUENCER

After the music has been recorded into the sequencer, you should be able to hear your performance when you activate the playback function. If you cannot get the sequencer to play back your performance, look at the sequencer's **memory status display.** The memory status display indicates how much computer memory has been used by your music. On some sequencers, however, the memory status display indicates the amount of memory available rather than the amount of memory used. If the amount of memory available is 100%, the MIDI data from your keyboard was not recorded. Retrace your steps using the following check list:

* If you are using an external sequencer, be sure that the synthesizer's MIDI OUT port is connected to the sequencer's MIDI IN port.
* Be sure that the sequencer track is set to record MIDI data on the same channel as the MIDI transmission channel on the synthesizer. For our example, both components should be set to Channel 5.
* Be sure that the sequencer is in record mode before you begin to play. On some sequencers, you can hear the metronome even though the sequencer is not recording.
* Check your connections. Try using a different MIDI cable from the synthesizer's MIDI OUT port to the sequencer's MIDI IN port.

If the amount of memory available is *less* than 100%, the MIDI data from your keyboard was recorded. The MIDI data, however, is not getting back to the synthesizer. Check the following:

* Be sure that the sequencer's MIDI OUT port is connected to the synthesizer's MIDI IN port.
* Be sure that the sequencer begins at measure 1 for playback.
* Check your connections. Try using a different MIDI cable from the sequencer's MIDI OUT port to the synthesizer's MIDI IN port.

BASIC SEQUENCER PLAYBACK FEATURES

Listed below are several playback features which are available on most sequencers. Be sure that you can perform each of the following operations on your sequencer.

1. **Change the playback tempo of the song.** You should be able to play your sequence at a variety of tempos. On most sequencers you can change the playback tempo by placing the cursor on the tempo display line and then typing in the desired tempo value. Some sequencers let you change the tempo while the music is playing. This is usually accomplished either by typing in the new tempo while the sequencer is playing (for an instantaneous tempo change), or by pressing the "+" or "-" keys (for a gradual tempo change).

2. **Pause in the middle of the song.** You should be able to stop the sequencer at any point in a song. You should also be able to continue the song playback from the stop point. On most sequencers you press the button labeled "START/STOP". If you press the START/STOP button when the sequencer is playing, the sequencer will stop. If you press the START/STOP button after the sequencer has stopped, the sequence will continue playing from the point at which it was stopped. For example, suppose you stopped the sequencer on Measure 18 of a sequence. When you press the START/STOP button, the sequence will begin at Measure 18.

3. **Start playback from any measure in a song.** This feature is especially useful when you are using the sequencer as a rehearsal aid. On most synthesizers, you simply type in the measure number where you want to start.

4. **Change the track program number.** By changing the track program number on the sequencer, you should be able to select different sounds without touching your synthesizer. Some sequencers allow you to change programs while the music is playing. This feature makes it very easy to select the most appropriate sound for any musical part. On most sequencers program changes are accomplished by placing the cursor on the program number line and then using the "+" or "-" buttons to step up or down through the program numbers.

5. **Transpose the track.** Most sequencers allow you to transpose tracks to any key. This is usually accomplished by placing the cursor on the transpose value (usually set to "0"), and by typing in the transposition value. For example, a transposition value of "+2" means that the music will be transposed two semitones higher. A transposition value of "-12" equals means that the music will be transposed 12 semitones (1 octave) lower.

6. **Loop the track.** When the loop feature is activated, a track will play through once, then repeat endlessly. Be sure you know how to activate and de-activate this feature. Some sequencers allow you to loop a specific measure or group of measures anywhere within a song. To do this, you must specify the starting measure number and the ending measure number of the loop.

7. **Mute the track.** The mute feature does not erase or destroy a track. Instead, it silences a track without the need to lower the track volume level. This feature is useful when you have recorded several tracks and want to hear only a specified number of tracks. For example, if you mute Track 1 in this lesson you will hear nothing since Track 1 contains all of the music.

8. **Solo the track.** The solo feature enables you to hear only one track. This feature is useful when you want to listen to only one track in a sequence that contains many tracks.

Chapter 4

HOW TO CREATER A MULTI-TRACK SEQUENCE

In Chapter 3 you learned how to create a single-track sequence. In this chapter you will learn how to create a **multi-track** sequence. A multi-track sequence uses several sequencer tracks, but all of the tracks play back using the same sound.

In Part 1, you will learn how to create a multi-track setup chart that will serve as your master plan before you begin to record. In Part 2, you will learn how to use the information in the setup chart to record a multi-track sequence.

PART 1 - CREATING A SETUP CHART

Step 1: Decide what you want to record.
You can record any kind of music using any sounds that you like. For this lesson, however, let's assume that you want to record the chorale in *Fig. 4.1*.

Fig. 4.1 A Mighty Fortress (harmonized by J.S. Bach)

Step 2: Decide on the number of tracks that you will need.
There are four parts in the chorale. Suppose that you want to record each part one at a time. In order to do this, you will need to use four separate tracks on the sequencer.

Step 3: Decide on the order in which you will record the parts.
You can choose to record any part first; for this example, start with the soprano part and record each line in descending order - alto, tenor, bass.

Step 4: Make a setup chart to list the information that you will need when begin to record the sequence.

In *Fig. 4.2*, you will see a partially completed setup chart that will help you keep track of the information needed to create a multi-track sequence. The first column lists the names of the 4 sequencer tracks that you will use in this lesson. The remaining columns will be completed as you select and reserve sequencer tracks, MIDI channels, and synthesizer programs to use in the recording process explained in Part 2 of this chapter.

SETUP CHART

	For External Sequencers				
Sequencer Track Name	Synthesizer MIDI Channel	Synthesizer Program Name	Synthesizer Program Number	Sequencer Track Number	Sequencer Track MIDI Channel
Soprano					
Alto					
Tenor					
Bass					

Fig. 4.2

Step 5: If you are using an external sequencer, select and reserve a MIDI channel on the synthesizer to be used for each musical part in the sequence.

Note: If you are using an integrated sequencer, skip this step.

You can use any MIDI channel, but for this lesson reserve MIDI Channel 5. Remember, all four parts will use the same synthesizer channel. Put this information in the setup chart. See *Fig. 4.3*.

SETUP CHART

	For External Sequencers				
Sequencer Track Name	Synthesizer MIDI Channel	Synthesizer Program Name	Synthesizer Program Number	Sequencer Track Number	Sequencer Track MIDI Channel
Soprano	(5)				
Alto	(5)				
Tenor	(5)				
Bass	(5)				

Fig. 4.3

42

Step 6: Select and reserve a program number on the synthesizer.

Suppose that you want to hear the chorale played with a pipe organ sound, and suppose that the program number for the pipe organ sound is 28. Reserve Program 28 on the synthesizer. Remember, all four parts will use the same pipe organ sound (Program 28). See *Fig. 4.4*.

SETUP CHART

	For External Sequencers				
Sequencer Track Name	Synthesizer MIDI Channel	Synthesizer Program Name	Synthesizer Program Number	Sequencer Track Number	Sequencer Track MIDI Channel
Soprano	(5)	**Pipe Organ**	**28**		
Alto	(5)	**Pipe Organ**	**28**		
Tenor	(5)	**Pipe Organ**	**28**		
Bass	(5)	**Pipe Organ**	**28**		

Fig. 4.4

Step 7: Select and reserve a sequencer track number for each instrumental part.

You can select any track. For this example, select track numbers as follows:

Musical Part	Sequencer Track Number
Soprano	Track 1
Alto	Track 2
Tenor	Track 3
Bass	Track 4

Put this information into the setup chart. See *Fig. 4.5*.

SETUP CHART

	For External Sequencers				
Sequencer Track Name	Synthesizer MIDI Channel	Synthesizer Program Name	Synthesizer Program Number	Sequencer Track Number	Sequencer Track MIDI Channel
Soprano	(5)	Pipe Organ	28	1	
Alto	(5)	Pipe Organ	28	2	
Tenor	(5)	Pipe Organ	28	3	
Bass	(5)	Pipe Organ	28	4	

Fig. 4.5

Step 8: Reserve the appropriate sequencer MIDI channel for each track.

If you are using an external sequencer, you have already reserved MIDI Channel 5 for the synthesizer (See Step 5). Now reserve Channel 5 for Tracks 1, 2, 3, and 4 on the sequencer. When recording with an external sequencer, remember that synthesizer channel numbers and sequencer track channel numbers should match.

Synthesizer MIDI Channels	Sequencer Track MIDI Channels
Soprano Part - MIDI Channel 5	Track 1 - MIDI Channel 5
Alto Part - MIDI Channel 5	Track 2 - MIDI Channel 5
Tenor Part - MIDI Channel 5	Track 3 - MIDI Channel 5
Bass Part - MIDI Channel 5	Track 4 - MIDI Channel 5

Put this information in the setup chart. See *Fig. 4.6.*

SETUP CHART

For External
Sequencers

Sequencer Track Name	Synthesizer MIDI Channel	Synthesizer Program Name	Synthesizer Program Number	Sequencer Track Number	Sequencer Track MIDI Channel
Soprano	(5)	Pipe Organ	28	1	**5**
Alto	(5)	Pipe Organ	28	2	**5**
Tenor	(5)	Pipe Organ	28	3	**5**
Bass	(5)	Pipe Organ	28	4	**5**

Fig. 4.6

Now the setup chart is complete. Refer to it whenever you are ready to record each track of the chorale. For your convenience, you will find a duplicate setup chart (*Fig. 4.6*) on p.153 that you may remove for easy reference when you record the chorale.

PART 2 - RECORDING A MULTI-TRACK SEQUENCE

Step 1: Make sure that the synthesizer and sequencer are turned on.

When you play the synthesizer, you should be able to hear its sound either through speakers or through headphones.

Step 2: If you are using an external sequencer, set up the MIDI connections between the sequencer and the multi-timbralsynthesizer.

> *Note: If you are using an integrated sequencer, skip this step.*

If you are using either a hardware or software sequencer, use one MIDI cable to connect the MIDI OUT port of the synthesizer to the MIDI IN port of the sequencer. Use another MIDI cable to connect the MIDI OUT port of the sequencer to the MIDI IN port of the synthesizer. Your MIDI connections should look like the connections shown in *Fig. 4.7*.

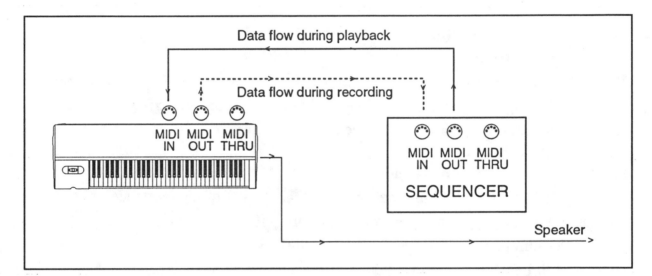

Fig. 4.7 - The proper MIDI connections between a synthesizer and an external sequencer.

Step 3: If you are using an integrated sequencer, enter the sequencer mode.

> *Note: If you are using an external sequencer, skip this step.*

On most instruments the sequencer mode can be activated by pressing a button labeled "SEQ" or "SEQUENCER". Consult your owner's manual to learn how to enter the sequencer mode of your instrument.

Step 4: Set the song tempo.
The music to be recorded in *Fig. 4.1* has a metronome marking of 80 *bpm* (*beats per minute*). Set your song tempo indicator to this value. If you can't play the

music at the indicated tempo, choose a slower tempo for the recording process. Be sure to change the tempo to the original value when you have finished recording. For example, if you feel more comfortable playing the parts at a metronome marking of 50 *bpm*, set the tempo indicator at 50 *bpm* and record the parts at this tempo. After you finish recording, change the tempo indicator to 80 *bpm* and the sequencer will play back at the correct tempo.

Step 5: Set the time signature.

On most sequencers, you can enter the time signature by first locating the time signature on the sequencer screen and then entering the desired time signature. In this exercise, you would type "4" twice.

Step 6: Set the note (or record) resolution value to the highest resolution.

You will learn about sequencer resolution in Chapter 8. For now, set the resolution value to the highest resolution. The highest resolution will give you the most accurate playback of your performance.

Step 7: Activate the metronome.

Since you will be overdubbing the remaining three parts of the sequence, you should use the metronome when recording each part. If your sequencer allows you to specify the number of clicks per measure, adjust the metronome so that it clicks on every eighth beat. Be sure that your synthesizer sound is soft enough for you to be able to hear the clicks at all times.

Step 8: Set the number of lead-in measures for the metronome.

A lead-in measure allows you to hear one measure of metronome clicks before the sequencer begins recording. On some sequencers, it is possible to vary the number of lead-in measures. A one measure lead-in should work for this sequence.

Step 9: If you are using an external sequencer, assign the MIDI Channel number on the synthesizer to the appropriate channel number.

> *Note: If you are using an integrated sequencer, skip this step.*

In the setup chart (*Fig. 4.6*), you reserved MIDI channel 5 for the synthesizer. The MIDI channel setting on most synthesizers is usually found in the "UTILITIES", "GLOBAL", or "MIDI" section of the instrument. (Consult your owner's manual to learn how to change the MIDI channel.)

Step 10: Assign Track 1 to the appropriate MIDI channel.
In the setup chart (*Fig. 4.6*), you reserved MIDI Channel 5 for Track 1. Place the sequencer cursor on the line that designates the MIDI channel for Track 1 and set the channel number to 5.

Step 11: If you are using an external sequencer, turn off the "MIDI ECHO" or "MIDI THRU" function on the sequencer.

Note: If you are using an integrated sequencer, skip this step.

If MIDI THRU is activated, the sequencer will send any incoming MIDI data through the sequencer's MIDI OUT port. When you play a note on the keyboard, the synthesizer will play two identical notes. The synthesizer's microprocessor (or "brain") receives two commands to play the same note. One command comes from the keyboard and another command from the sequencer. This doubling of every note changes the tone quality of certain sounds. It also reduces the number of notes that can be played simultaneously. For example, if your instrument is normally capable of playing 16 notes simultaneously, it will be capable of playing only 8 notes simultaneously under these conditions.

Step 12: Assign the sound for the first track on the sequencer.
In the setup chart (*Fig. 4.6*), you selected the pipe organ sound (Program 28) for all of the instrumental parts. Place the sequencer cursor on the program number line for Track 1 and enter the number 28. (Be sure that Program 28 is selected on the synthesizer.)

Step 13: Identify the contents of the first track with a name.
If your sequencer allows you to name an empty track, place the cursor on the name line for Track 1 and type the word "Soprano".

Step 14: Identify the sequence with a name.
If your sequencer allows you to name a song, place the cursor on the song title line and type the name "Fortress". Your sequencer screen should now look something like *Fig. 4.8* on p.48.

SONG NAME: Fortress			**TIME SIG:** 4/4
SONG TEMPO: 80	**MIDI ECHO:** Off		**METRONOME:** On

TRACK	NAME	MIDI CHANNEL	PROGRAM
1	Soprano	5	28
2	___	—	—
3	___	—	—
4	___	—	—
5	___	—	—
6	___	—	—
7	___	—	—
8	___	—	—

Fig 4.8

Step 15: Record the first musical part of the multi-track sequence.

Now you are ready to record the first track of the sequence. See *Fig. 4.9.*

Fig. 4.9. Soprano part

On most sequencers, you begin recording by pressing a button labeled "RECORD", "REC", or "START". While you are recording the soprano part, you will hear the sound of the metronome from the sequencer. The metronome is not being recorded.

Step 16: Select a different sequencer track for the second musical part.

You can select any empty track, but in the setup chart (*Fig. 4.6*), you reserved Track 2. On most sequencers you select a different track by placing the cursor on the line that designates the desired track. (Consult your owner's manual to learn how to record on different tracks.)

Step 17: Assign the second track of the sequence to the same MIDI channel used for Track 1.

Assign Track 2 to the same MIDI channel used by Track 1 (Channel 5). In this way, the alto part will be heard using the same sound that was used for the soprano part. Place the sequencer cursor on the line that designates the MIDI channel number for Track 2 and set the channel number to 5. It's not necessary to enter the program number for Track 2 because this value was entered on Track 1. Note: A MIDI channel can be assigned only one program number at a time.

Step 18: Identify the contents of the second track with a name.

If your sequencer allows you to name a track, place the cursor on the name line and type the word "Alto". The sequencer screen should now look something like *Fig. 4.10*.

SONG NAME: Fortress		TIME SIG: 4/4	
SONG TEMPO: 80	MIDI ECHO: Off	METRONOME: On	
TRACK	NAME	MIDI CHANNEL	PROGRAM
1	Soprano	5	28
2	Alto	5	—
3		—	—
4		—	—
5		—	—
6		—	—
7		—	—
8		—	—

Fig. 4.10

Step 19: Record the second musical part of the multi-track sequence.

At this point, you're ready to record the second part - the alto part. While you are recording on Track 2, you will hear the soprano part on Track 1 and the metronome. When you finish recording the alto part, you will have two musical parts recorded on two separate tracks. When you play back the sequence, you will hear the music in *Fig. 4.11*.

Fig. 4.11 Soprano and alto parts

Step 20: Select a different track for the third musical part.

You can select any empty track, but in the setup chart (*Fig. 4.6*) you selected Track 3.

Step 21: Assign the third track of the sequence to the same MIDI channel used
for Track 1 and Track 2.

Assign Track 3 to MIDI Channel 5. Refer to the setup chart (*Fig. 4.6*).

Step 22: Identify the contents of the third track with a name.

Place the cursor on the name line for Track 3 and type the word "Tenor". Your sequencer screen should now look something like *Fig. 4.12*.

SONG NAME: Fortress			TIME SIG: 4/4
SONG TEMPO: 80	MIDI ECHO: Off		METRONOME: On
TRACK	NAME	MIDI CHANNEL	PROGRAM
1	Soprano	5	28
2	Alto	5	—
3	Tenor	5	—
4		—	—
5		—	—
6		—	—
7		—	—
8		—	—

Fig. 4.12

Step 23: Record the third musical part of the multi-track sequence.

Now you are ready to record on Track 3. While you are recording on Track 3, you will hear the alto part on Track 2, the soprano part on Track 1, and the metronome.

When you finish recording the tenor part, you will have three musical parts recorded on three separate tracks. When you play back the sequence, you should hear the music in *Fig. 4.13*.

Fig. 4.13 Soprano, alto & tenor parts

Step 24: Select a different track for the fourth musical part.
You can select any empty track, but in the setup chart (*Fig. 4.6*, p.44) you reserved Track 4.

Step 25: Assign the fourth track of the sequence to the same sequencer MIDI channel used for Track 1, Track 2, and Track 3.
Assign Track 4 to MIDI Channel 5. Refer to the setup chart (*Fig. 4.6*).

Step 26: Identify the contents of the fourth track with a name.
Place the cursor on the name line for Track 4 and type the word "Bass". Your sequencer screen should now look something like *Fig. 4.14*.

| SONG NAME: Fortress | | | TIME SIG: 4/4 |
| SONG TEMPO: 80 | MIDI ECHO: Off | | METRONOME: On |
TRACK	NAME	MIDI CHANNEL	PROGRAM
1	Soprano	5	28
2	Alto	5	—
3	Tenor	5	—
4	Bass	5	—
5		—	—
6		—	—
7		—	—
8		—	—

Fig. 4.14

Step 27: Record the fourth musical part of the multi-track sequence.

While you are recording on Track 4, you will hear the tenor part on Track 3, the alto part on Track 2, the soprano part on Track 1, and the metronome. When you finish recording the bass part, you will have four musical parts recorded on four separate sequencer tracks. When you play the sequence, you should hear the music in *Fig. 4.15*.

Fig. 4.15

Remember, all four musical parts are set to MIDI channel 5. This means that all four parts will be heard with the same sound - the sound of a pipe organ. If you want to use a sound other than a pipe organ sound, simply change the program number of Track 1 to some other number. All four parts will then be played with the same new sound. In the next two chapters, you will learn how to create a multi-timbral sequence by giving each musical part a different instrumental sound.

Chapter 5

HOW TO CREATE A MULTI-TIMBRAL SEQUENCE USING A MULTI-TIMBRAL SYNTHESIZER

In Chapter 4 you learned how to create a multi-track sequence - a sequence containing several tracks with all of the tracks assigned to the same MIDI channel and using the same program (sound). In this chapter, you will learn how to create a **multi-timbral** sequence -a sequence using several tracks, with each track assigned to a different MIDI channel and with each track using a different program.

To create a multi-timbral sequence using one synthesizer, you must have a **multi-timbral synthesizer**. A multi-timbral synthesizer is an instrument that can play different programs on different MIDI channels at the same time. In other words, a multi-timbral synthesizer can function as several mono-timbral synthesizers. Most multi-timbral synthesizers allow you to set up multi-timbral combinations to specify 1) the number of different timbres that you will use; 2) the MIDI channel for each timbre; and 3) the program number for each timbre.

To learn how to create a multi-timbral sequence using one multi-timbral synthesizer, follow the steps in Part 1 and Part 2. In Part 1, you will learn how to create a setup chart that will serve as your master plan before you begin to record. In Part 2, you will learn how to use the information in the setup chart to record a multi-timbral sequence.

PART 1 - CREATING A SETUP CHART

Step 1: Decide what you want to record.
You can record any kind of music using any sounds that you like. For this lesson, however, let's assume that you want to record the chorale in *Fig. 5.1*.

Fig. 5.1. A Mighty Fortress (harmonized by J.S. Bach)

Step 2: Decide on the number of synthesizer timbres and sequencer tracks that you will need.

There are four parts in the chorale. In order to hear four different instrumental sounds, you will need to use four different synthesizer timbres and four separate sequencer tracks.

Step 3: Decide on the order in which you will record the parts.

You can choose to record any part first; however for this exercise, start with the soprano part and record each line in descending order - soprano, alto , tenor, bass.

Step 4: Make a setup chart to list the information that you will need when you begin to record the sequence.

In *Fig. 5.2*, you will see a partially completed setup chart that will help you to keep track of the information that you will need to create a multi-timbral sequence. The first column lists the names of the four sequencer tracks that you will use in this exercise. The remaining columns will be completed as you select and reserve sequencer tracks, MIDI channels, and synthesizer programs to use in the recording process outlined in Part 2 of this chapter.

SETUP CHART

Sequencer Track Name	Synthesizer Timbre Number	For External Sequencers Synthesizer Timbre MIDI Channel	Synthesizer Program Name	Synthesizer Program Number	Sequencer Track Number	Sequencer Track MIDI Channel
Soprano						
Alto						
Tenor						
Bass						

Fig. 5.2

54

Step 5: Select a synthesizer timbre number for each musical part.

Reserve the following synthesizer timbres for the 4 musical parts:

Musical Part	Synthesizer Timbre Number
Soprano	Timbre 1
Alto	Timbre 2
Tenor	Timbre 3
Bass	Timbre 4

The setup chart will now look like *Fig. 5.3*.

SETUP CHART

Sequencer Track Name	Synthesizer Timbre Number	Synthesizer Timbre MIDI Channel	Synthesizer Program Name	Synthesizer Program Number	Sequencer Track Number	Sequencer Track MIDI Channel
		For External Sequencers				
Soprano	1					
Alto	2					
Tenor	3					
Bass	4					

Fig. 5.3

Step 6: If you are using an external sequencer, select and reserve a MIDI channel for each synthesizer timbre.

Note: If you are using an integrated sequencer, skip this step.

The chorale uses four different instrumental sounds; therefore, you will need to use four different timbres on the synthesizer. You will also need to use four different MIDI channels. You can use any four MIDI channels, but for this example reserve the channels as follows:

SYNTHESIZER TIMBRE	MIDI CHANNEL
Timbre 1 (Soprano)	5
Timbre 2 (Alto)	6
Timbre 3 (Tenor)	7
Timbre 4 (Bass)	8

Make sure that the synthesizer's master MIDI channel setting is not set to a MIDI channel used by the synthesizer timbres. In other words, set the instrument's master MIDI channel to any channel except channels 5, 6, 7, or 8. The setup chart will now look like *Fig. 5.4*.

SETUP CHART

| | | For External Sequencers | | | | |
Sequencer Track Name	Synthesizer Timbre Number	Synthesizer Timbre MIDI Channel	Synthesizer Program Name	Synthesizer Program Number	Sequencer Track Number	Sequencer Track MIDI Channel
Soprano	1	(5)				
Alto	2	(6)				
Tenor	3	(7)				
Bass	4	(8)				

Fig. 5.4

Step 7: Select and reserve a program number for each synthesizer timbre.

You can select any instrumental sounds that you think are appropriate, but for the chorale used in *Fig. 5.1*, select and reserve the programs as follows:

Synthesizer Timbre	Program Name	Program Number
Timbre 1 (Soprano)	Flute	24
Timbre 2 (Alto)	Oboe	13
Timbre 3 (Tenor)	Clarinet	47
Timbre 4 (Bass)	Bassoon	11

The setup chart will now look like *Fig. 5.5*.

SETUP CHART

| | | For External Sequencers | | | | |
Sequencer Track Name	Synthesizer Timbre Number	Synthesizer Timbre MIDI Channel	Synthesizer Program Name	Synthesizer Program Number	Sequencer Track Number	Sequencer Track MIDI Channel
Soprano	1	(5)	Flute	24		
Alto	2	(6)	Oboe	13		
Tenor	3	(7)	Clarinet	47		
Bass	4	(8)	Bassoon	11		

Fig. 5.5

Step 8: Select and reserve a sequencer track number for each synthesizer timbre.

You can select any track number, but for this example reserve the track numbers as follows:

Synthesizer Timbre	Sequencer Track Number
Timbre 1 (Soprano)	Track 1
Timbre 2 (Alto)	Track 2
Timbre 3 (Tenor)	Track 3
Timbre 4 (Bass)	Track 4

The setup chart will now look like *Fig. 5.6.*

SETUP CHART

Sequencer Track Name	Synthesizer Timbre Number	Synthesizer Timbre MIDI Channel	Synthesizer Program Name	Synthesizer Program Number	Sequencer Track Number	Sequencer Track MIDI Channel
		For External Sequencers				
Soprano	1	(5)	Flute	24	1	
Alto	2	(6)	Oboe	13	2	
Tenor	3	(7)	Clarinet	47	3	
Bass	4	(8)	Bassoon	11	4	

Fig. 5.6

Step 9: Select and reserve the appropriate sequencer MIDI channel for each track.

If you are using an external sequencer, you already reserved a MIDI channel for each synthesizer timbre. (See Step 6 on p. 51.) Match the synthesizer timbre MIDI channel numbers to the MIDI channel numbers on sequencer tracks 1 - 4 as follows:

Synthesizer Timbre MIDI Channels	Sequencer Track MIDI Channels
Timbre 1 (Soprano) - Channel 5	Track 1 - Channel 5
Timbre 2 (Alto) - Channel 6	Track 2 - Channel 6
Timbre 3 (Tenor) - Channel 7	Track 3 - Channel 7
Timbre 4 (Bass) - Channel 8	Track 4 - Channel 8

Remember that synthesizer channel numbers and sequencer track channel numbers should match. The setup chart will now look like *Fig. 5.7*.

SETUP CHART

Sequencer Track Name	Synthesizer Timbre Number	For External Sequencers Synthesizer Timbre MIDI Channel	Synthesizer Program Name	Synthesizer Program Number	Sequencer Track Number	Sequencer Track MIDI Channel
Soprano	1	(5)	Flute	24	1	**5**
Alto	2	(6)	Oboe	13	2	**6**
Tenor	3	(7)	Clarinet	47	3	**7**
Bass	4	(8)	Bassoon	11	4	**8**

Fig. 5.7

Now the setup chart is complete. You should refer to it whenever you are ready to record each track of the chorale. For your convenience, you will find a duplicate setup chart (*Fig. 5.7*) on p.153 that you may remove for easy reference when you record the chorale.

PART 2 - RECORDING A MULTI-TIMBRAL SEQUENCE

Step 1: Make sure that the synthesizer and the sequencer are turned on.
When you play the synthesizer, you should be able to hear its sound either through speakers or through headphones. If you are using an external sequencer, make sure that it is on.

Step 2: If you are using an external sequencer, set up the MIDI connections between the sequencer and the multi-timbral synthesizer.

> *Note: If you are using an integrated sequencer, skip this step.*

If you are using an external sequencer, your MIDI connections should look like the connections shown in *Fig. 5.8*.

58

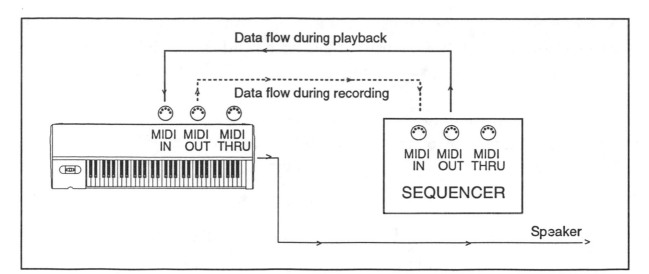

Figure 5.8 - The proper MIDI connections between a synthesizer and an external sequencer.

Step 3: If you are using an external sequencer, enter the multi-timbral mode on your synthesizer.

Note: If you are using an integrated sequencer, skip this step.

The multi-timbral section on synthesizers is usually accessed by pressing a button labeled "MULTI" or "COMBI". (Consult your owner's manual to learn how to enter the multi-timbral mode on your instrument.)

Step 4: If you are using an integrated sequencer, enter the sequencer mode.

Note: If you are using an external sequencer, skip this step.

On most instruments this is accomplished by pressing a button labeled "SEQ" or "SEQUENCER". Consult your owner's manual to learn how to enter the sequencer mode of your instrument.

Step 5: Set the song tempo.
The music to be recorded in *Fig. 5.1* has a metronome marking of 80 *bpm* (*beats per minute*). Set your song tempo indicator to this value. If you can't play the music at the indicated tempo, choose a slower tempo for the recording process. Be sure to change the tempo to the original value when you have finished recording. For example, if you

feel more comfortable playing the parts at a metronome marking of 50 *bpm*, set the tempo indicator at 50 *bpm* and record the parts at this tempo. After you finish recording, change the tempo indicator to 80 *bpm*, and the sequencer will play back at the correct tempo.

Step 6: Set the time signature.

On most sequencers, you can enter the time signature by first locating the time signature on the sequencer screen and then entering the desired time signature. In this exercise, you would type "4" twice.

Step 7: Set the note (or record) resolution value to the highest resolution.

You will learn about sequencer resolution in Chapter 8. For now, set the resolution value to the highest resolution. The highest resolution setting will give you the most accurate playback of your performance.

Step 8: Activate the metronome.

Since you will be overdubbing the remaining three parts of the sequence, you should use the metronome when recording each part. If your sequencer allows you to specify the number of clicks per measure, adjust the metronome so that it clicks on every eighth beat. Be sure that your synthesizer sound is soft enough so that you can hear the clicks at all times.

Step 9: Set the number of lead-in measures for the metronome.

A lead-in measure allows you to hear one measure of metronome clicks before the sequencer begins recording. On some sequencers, it is possible to vary the number of lead-in measures. A one measure lead-in should work well for this sequence.

Step 10: If you are using an external sequencer, assign Synthesizer Timbre 1 to the appropriate MIDI channel.

Note: If you are using an integrated sequencer, skip this step.

In the setup chart (*Fig. 5.7*), you reserved MIDI Channel 5 for Synthesizer Timbre 1 (Soprano). If you are using an external sequencer, consult your owner's manual to learn how to assign the MIDI channel for each timbre in a multi-timbral combination on your instrument.

Step 11:   Assign the MIDI channel for Sequencer Track 1 to the MIDI channel reserved for Synthesizer Timbre 1.

In the setup chart (*Fig. 5.7*), you reserved MIDI Channel 5 for Synthesizer Timbre 1 (Soprano). Place the sequencer cursor on the line that designates the MIDI channel for Track 1 and set the channel number to 5.

Step 12: Assign the sound for Track 1 on the sequencer.

In the setup chart (*Fig. 5.7*), you selected the flute sound (Program 24) for the soprano part (Timbre 1). Place the sequencer cursor on the program number line for Track 1 and enter the number 24.

Step 13: Set up the synthesizer so that you hear the sound of Timbre 1 when you play the keyboard.

You have already decided to record the soprano part first. Since Timbre 1 (flute) is set to MIDI Channel 5, you must be sure that your synthesizer is transmitting MIDI data into the sequencer on Channel 5. Change the instrument's master MIDI channel setting to Channel 5. This setting is usually found in the "UTILITIES", "GLOBAL", or "MIDI" section of the instrument. (Consult your owner's manual to learn how to play individual timbres in a multi-timbral setup on the keyboard). After you set the master MIDI channel to 5, you will hear only the flute sound when you play the keyboard.

Note: If you are using an integrated sequencer, you can usually play individual timbres by changing the highlighted track number in the display. For example, if Track 1 is highlighted in the display, you will hear the flute sound when you play the keyboard. If Track 2 is highlighted, you will hear a different sound when you play the keyboard. Consult your owner's manual to learn how to activate different tracks on an integrated sequencer.

Step 14: If you are using an external sequencer, turn off the "MIDI ECHO" or "MIDI THRU" function on the sequencer.

Note: If you are using an integrated sequencer, skip this step.

If MIDI THRU is activated, the sequencer will send any incoming MIDI data through the sequencer's MIDI OUT port. The synthesizer will play two identical notes whenever you play a note on the keyboard. The synthesizer's microprocessor (or "brain") receives a command to play a note from the keyboard and another command from the sequencer to play the same note. This doubling of every note can change the tone quality of certain sounds. It also reduces by half the number of notes that can be played simultaneously. For example, if your instrument is normally capable of playing 16 notes simultaneously, it will be capable of playing only 8 notes simultaneously under these conditions.

Step 15: Adjust the volume level of the sound.
Most multi-timbral synthesizers have a volume level setting for each timbre. (Some sequencers also have a volume level setting for each track.) Never record a sound at the maximum volume level because, when the need arises, it becomes impossible to make the sound louder. As a general rule, set the volume level at 80% of maximum level so that you will have room to decrease or to increase volume levels when needed.

Step 16: Identify the contents of the first track with a name.
If your sequencer allows you to name an empty track, place the cursor on the sequencer's name line for Track 1 and type the word "Soprano". Your sequencer screen should now look something like *Fig. 5.9.* (If your sequencer does not allow you to name an empty track, be sure to name the track as soon as you have recorded the part.)

SONG NAME: Fortress			TIME SIG: 4/4
SONG TEMPO: 80	MIDI ECHO: Off		METRONOME: On
TRACK	**NAME**	**MIDI CHANNEL**	**PROGRAM**
1	Soprano	5	24
2		–	–
3		–	–
4		–	–
5		–	–
6		–	–
7		–	–
8		–	–

Fig. 5.9

62

Step 17: Record the first part of the multi-timbral sequence.

Now you are ready to record the first track of the sequence. See *Fig. 5.10.*

Fig. 5.10 The soprano part.

On most sequencers you begin recording by pressing the space bar or by pressing a button labeled "RECORD", "REC", or "START". While you are recording the soprano part, you will hear the sound of the metronome from the sequencer. The metronome is not being recorded.

Step 18: Select a different sequencer track for the second musical part.
You can select any empty track, but in the setup chart (*Fig. 5.7*) you reserved Track 2. On most sequencers you select a different track by placing the cursor on the line that designates the desired track. (Consult your owner's manual to learn how to record on different tracks.)

Step 19: If you are using an external sequencer, assign Synthesizer Timbre 2 to MIDI Channel 6.

Note: If you are using an integrated sequencer, skip this step.

In the setup chart (*Fig. 5.7*), you reserved MIDI Channel 6 for Synthesizer Timbre 2 (Alto). If you are using either a hardware or a software sequencer, consult your owner's manual to learn how to assign the MIDI channel for each timbre in a multi-timbral combination on your instrument.

Step 20: Assign the MIDI channel for Sequencer Track 2 to the MIDI channel reserved for Synthesizer Timbre 2.
In the setup chart (*Fig. 5.7*), you reserved MIDI Channel 6 for Synthesizer Timbre 2 (Alto). Place the sequencer cursor on the line that designates the MIDI channel for Track 2 and set the channel number to 6.

Step 21: Select the desired sound for the second track on the sequencer.

The alto part uses the oboe sound (Program 13). Place the sequencer's cursor on the program number line for Track 2 and enter the number 13.

Step 22: Adjust the volume level of the sound.

Adjust the volume levels so that you have a balance between the flute sound on Track 1 and the oboe sound you will be recording on Track 2.

Step 23: Identify the contents of the second track with a name.

If your sequencer allows you to name an empty track, place the cursor on the name line for Track 2 and type the word "Alto". Your sequencer screen should look something like *Fig. 5.11*.

SONG NAME: Fortress SONG TEMPO: 80		MIDI ECHO: Off	TIME SIG: 4/4 METRONOME: On
TRACK	**NAME**	**MIDI CHANNEL**	**PROGRAM**
1	Soprano	5	24
2	Alto	6	13
3		–	–
4		–	–
5		–	–
6		–	–
7		–	–
8		–	–

Fig. 5.11

Step 24: Record the second part of the multi-timbral sequence.

At this point, you are ready to record the alto part. While you are recording on Track 2, you will hear the soprano part on Track 1 and the metronome. When you finish recording the alto part, you will have two musical parts recorded on two separate tracks. When you play back the sequence, you will hear the music in *Fig. 5.12*.

Fig. 5.12 Soprano and alto parts

Step 25:   Select a different sequencer track for the third musical part.
You can select any empty track, but for this exercise select Track 3.

Step 26: If you are using an external sequencer, assign Synthesizer Timbre 3 to MIDI Channel 7.

Note: If you are using an integrated sequencer, skip this step.

In the setup chart (*Fig. 5.7*), you reserved MIDI Channel 7 for Synthesizer Timbre 3 (Tenor). If you are using either a hardware or a software sequencer, consult your owner's manual to learn how to assign the MIDI channel for each timbre in a multi-timbral combination on your instrument.

Step 27:   Assign the MIDI channel for Sequencer Track 3 to the same MIDI channel reserved for Synthesizer Timbre 3.
In the setup chart (*Fig. 5.7*), you reserved MIDI channel 7 for Synthesizer Timbre 3 (Tenor). Place the sequencer cursor on the line that designates the MIDI channel for Track 3 and set the channel number to 7.

Step 28: Select the desired sound for the third track on the sequencer.
The tenor part uses the clarinet sound (Program 47). Place the sequencer's cursor on the program number line for Track 3 and enter the number 47.

Step 29: Adjust the volume level of the sound.
Adjust the volume levels so that you have a balance between the flute sound on Track 1, the oboe sound on Track 2, and the clarinet sound that you will be recording on Track 3.

Step 30:   Identify the contents of the third sequencer track with a name.
If your sequencer allows you to name an empty track, place the cursor on the name line for Track 3 and type the word "Tenor". Your sequencer screen should now look something like *Fig. 5.13*.

| SONG NAME: Fortress | | TIME SIG: 4/4 | |
| SONG TEMPO: 80 | MIDI ECHO: Off | METRONOME: On | |

TRACK	NAME	MIDI CHANNEL	PROGRAM
1	Soprano	5	24
2	Alto	6	13
3	Tenor	7	47
4		—	—
5		—	—
6		—	—
7		—	—
8		—	—

Fig. 5.13

Step 31: Record the third part of the multi-timbral sequence.

Now you are ready to record the tenor part. While you are recording on Track 3, you will hear the alto part on Track 2, the soprano part on Track 1, and the metronome. When you finish recording the tenor part, you will have three musical parts recorded on three separate tracks. When you play back the sequence, you should hear the music in *Fig. 5.14.*

Fig. 5.14 Soprano, alto and tenor parts

Step 32: Select a different sequencer track for the fourth musical part.

You can record the bassoon part on any empty track, but for this sequence select Track 4.

Step 33: If you are using an external sequencer, assign Synthesizer Timbre 4 to MIDI Channel 8.

Note: If you are using an integrated sequencer, skip this step.

66

In the setup chart (*Fig. 5.7*), you reserved MIDI Channel 8 for Synthesizer Timbre 4 (Bass). Consult your owner's manual to learn how to assign the MIDI channel for each timbre in a multi-timbral combination on your instrument.

Step 34: Assign the MIDI channel of Sequencer Track 4 of the sequencer to the same MIDI channel used for Synthesizer Timbre 4.

In the setup chart (*Fig. 5.7*), you reserved MIDI channel 8 for Synthesizer Timbre 4 (Bass). Place the sequencer cursor on the line that designates the MIDI channel for Track 4 and set the channel number to 8.

Step 35: Select the desired sound for the fourth track on the sequencer.

The bass part uses the bassoon sound (Program 11). Place the sequencer cursor on the program number line for Track 4 and enter the number 11.

Step 36: If possible, use the sequencer to adjust the volume level of the sound.

If your sequencer has a volume level setting for each track, adjust the volume levels so that you have a balance between the flute sound on Track 1, the oboe sound on Track 2, the clarinet sound on Track 3, and the bassoon sound you will be recording on Track 4.

Step 37: Identify the contents of the fourth sequencer track with a name.

If your sequencer allows you to name an empty track, place the sequencer cursor on the name line for Track 4 and type the word "Bass". The sequencer screen should look something like *Fig. 5.15*.

SONG NAME: Fortress			**TIME SIG: 4/4**
SONG TEMPO: 80	**MIDI ECHO: Off**		**METRONOME: On**
TRACK	**NAME**	**MIDI CHANNEL**	**PROGRAM**
1	Soprano	5	24
2	Alto	6	13
3	Tenor	7	47
4	Bass	8	11
5		–	–
6		–	–
7		–	–
8		–	–

Fig. 5.15

Step 38: Record the fourth part of the multi-timbral sequence.

While you are recording on Track 4, you will hear the tenor part on Track 3, the alto part on Track 2, the soprano part on Track 1, and the metronome. When you finish recording the bass part, you will have four musical parts recorded on four separate tracks. When you play back the sequence, you should hear the music in *Fig. 5.16.*

Fig. 5.16. Soprano, alto, tenor, and bass parts

Chapter 6

HOW TO CREATE A MULTI-TIMBRAL SEQUENCE USING MONO-TIMBRAL SYNTHESIZERS

In Chapter 5 you learned how to create a multi-timbral sequence using a multi-timbral synthesizer. In this chapter, you will learn how to create a multi-timbral sequence using mono-timbral synthesizers.

Most older synthesizers are **mono-timbral** instruments that transmit and receive MIDI data on only one channel at a time. Because of this limitation, mono-timbral synthesizers can play only one sound at a time (a piano part, or a drum part, or a guitar part, etc.). If you want to create a sequence with four different sounds - for example flute, piano, bass, and drums - you will need four mono-timbral synthesizers with each synthesizer assigned to a different MIDI channel and each using a different program. To learn how to create a multi-timbral sequence using mono-timbral synthesizers, follow the steps listed below.

In Part 1, you will learn how to create a setup chart which will serve as your master plan before you begin to record. In Part 2 you will learn how to use the information in the setup chart to record a multi-timbral sequence.

PART 1 - CREATING A SETUP CHART

Step 1: Decide what you want to record.
Obviously you can record any kind of music using any sounds that you like. For this lesson, however, let's assume that you want to record the chorale in *Fig. 6.1*.

Fig. 6.1. A Mighty Fortress (harmonized by J.S. Bach)

Step 2: Decide on the number of synthesizer timbres and sequencer tracks that you will need.

There are four parts in the chorale. In order to hear four different instrumental sounds, you will need to use four different synthesizer timbres and four separate tracks on the sequencer.

Step 3: Decide on the order in which you will record the parts.

You can choose to record any part first; however for this exercise, start with the soprano part and record each line in descending order - soprano, alto, tenor, bass.

Step 4: Make a setup chart to list the information that you will need when you begin to record the sequence.

In *Fig. 6.2,* you will see a partially completed setup chart which will help you to keep track of the information needed to create a multi-timbral sequence. The first column lists the names of the 4 sequencer tracks that you will use in this exercise. The remaining columns will be completed as you select sequencer tracks, MIDI channels, and synthesizer programs to use in the recording process outlined in Part 2 of this chapter.

SETUP CHART

Sequencer Track Name	Instrument	Instrument Function	Instrument MIDI Channel	Instrument Program Name	Instrument Program Number	Sequencer Track Number	Sequencer Track MIDI Channel
Soprano							
Alto							
Tenor							
Bass							

Fig. 6.2

Step 5: Determine the function of each synthesizer in the setup.
The chorale uses four different instrumental sounds (timbres); therefore, you will need to use four different mono-timbral synthesizers. Any MIDI equipped synthesizer can function either as a **master keyboard** (an instrument which generates MIDI data) or as **a slave** (an instrument which receives MIDI data).

In the setup chart below, Synthesizer D has been designated as the master keyboard, and Synthesizers A, B, and C have been designated as the slave synthesizers. Synthesizer D (master keyboard) is used to enter MIDI data into the sequencer. In this setup, you will not play the slave keyboards manually; instead, they will be controlled by the master keyboard (when you are recording a part) or by the sequencer (when you are playing back parts). See *Fig. 6.3*.

SETUP CHART

Sequencer Track Name	Instrument	Instrument Function	Instrument MIDI Channel	Instrument Program Name	Instrument Program Number	Sequencer Track Number	Sequencer Track MIDI Channel
Soprano	Synthesizer A	Slave A					
Alto	Synthesizer B	Slave B					
Tenor	Synthesizer C	Slave C					
Bass	Synthesizer D	Master Keyboard					

Fig. 6.3

Step 6: Select and reserve a MIDI channel for each synthesizer.
The chorale uses four different instrumental sounds (timbres); therefore, you will need to use four different MIDI channels. You can use any four MIDI channels, but for this example reserve the channels as follows:

INSTRUMENT	MIDI CHANNEL
Slave A	Channel 5
Slave B	Channel 6
Slave C	Channel 7
Master Keyboard	Channel 8

See the setup chart in *Fig. 6.4*.

SETUP CHART

Sequencer Track Name	Instrument	Instrument Function	Instrument MIDI Channel	Instrument Program Name	Instrument Program Number	Sequencer Track Number	Sequencer Track MIDI Channel
Soprano	Synthesizer A	Slave A	5				
Alto	Synthesizer B	Slave B	6				
Tenor	Synthesizer C	Slave C	7				
Bass	Synthesizer D	Master Keyboard	8				

Fig. 6.4

Step 7: Select and reserve a program number for each synthesizer.

You can select any instrumental sounds that you think are appropriate, but for the chorale used in *Fig. 6.1*, select and reserve the programs as follows:

Instrument	Sound	Program Number
Slave A (Soprano)	Flute	24
Slave B (Alto)	Oboe	13
Slave C (Tenor)	Clarinet	47
Master Keyboard (Bass)	Bassoon	11

See the setup chart in *Fig. 6.5*.

SETUP CHART

Sequencer Track Name	Instrument	Instrument Function	Instrument MIDI Channel	Instrument Program Name	Instrument Program Number	Sequencer Track Number	Sequencer Track MIDI Channel
Soprano	Synthesizer A	Slave A	5	**Flute**	**24**		
Alto	Synthesizer B	Slave B	6	**Oboe**	**13**		
Tenor	Synthesizer C	Slave C	7	**Clarinet**	**47**		
Bass	Synthesizer D	Master Keyboard	8	**Bassoon**	**11**		

Fig. 6.5

Step 8: Select and reserve a sequencer track number for each musical part.

You can select any track number, but for this example reserve the track numbers as follows:

Musical Part	Sequencer Track Number
Soprano	Track 1
Alto	Track 2
Tenor	Track 3
Bass	Track 4

See the setup chart in *Fig. 6.6*.

SETUP CHART

Sequencer Track Name	Instrument	Instrument Function	Instrument MIDI Channel	Instrument Program Name	Instrument Program Number	Sequencer Track Number	Sequencer Track MIDI Channel
Soprano	Synthesizer A	Slave A	5	Flute	24	1	
Alto	Synthesizer B	Slave B	6	Oboe	13	2	
Tenor	Synthesizer C	Slave C	7	Clarinet	47	3	
Bass	Synthesizer D	Master Keyboard	8	Bassoon	11	4	

Fig. 6.6

Step 9: Reserve the appropriate sequencer MIDI channel for each track.

In Step 6, you reserved a MIDI channel for each synthesizer. Match the synthesizer MIDI channel numbers to the MIDI channel numbers on sequencer tracks 1-4 as follows:

Synthesizers	MIDI Channels	Sequencer Track	MIDI Channels
Slave A	5	Track 1	MIDI Channel 5
Slave B	6	Track 2	MIDI Channel 6
Slave C	7	Track 3	MIDI Channel 7
Master Keyboard	8	Track 4	MIDI Channel 8

Remember that synthesizer channel numbers and sequencer track channel numbers must match. See the setup chart in *Fig. 6.7*.

SETUP CHART

Sequencer Track Name	Instrument	Instrument Function	Instrument MIDI Channel	Instrument Program Name	Instrument Program Number	Sequencer Track Number	Sequencer Track MIDI Channel
Soprano	Synthesizer A	Slave A	5	Flute	24	1	5
Alto	Synthesizer B	Slave B	6	Oboe	13	2	6
Tenor	Synthesizer C	Slave C	7	Clarinet	47	3	7
Bass	Synthesizer D	Master Keyboard	8	Bassoon	11	4	8

Fig. 6.7

Now the setup chart is complete. You should refer to it whenever you are ready to record each track of the chorale. For your convenience, you will find a duplicate setup chart (*Fig. 6.7*) on p.153 which you may remove for reference when you record the chorale.

PART 2 - RECORDING A MULTI-TIMBRAL SEQUENCE

Step 1: Make sure that the synthesizers and the sequencer are turned on.

When you play each synthesizer, you should be able to hear its sound either through speakers or through headphones. If you are using an external sequencer, make sure that it is turned on.

Step 2: Set up the MIDI cable connections between the sequencer and the four synthesizers.

In Chapter 1, you learned the basic concepts of MIDI. Before you go any further in this chapter, you may want to review the concepts explained in Chapter 1. If you are using either a hardware or software sequencer, your MIDI connections should look like the connections shown in *Fig. 6.8*.

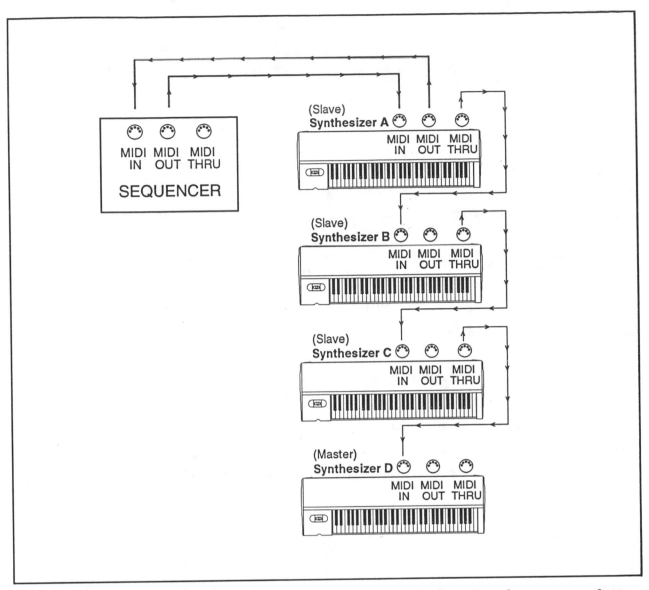

Fig. 6.8. The correct MIDI cable connections using either a hardware or software sequencer with four mono-timbral synthesizers.

In *Fig. 6.8* Synthesizer D (master keyboard) is used to enter MIDI data into the sequencer. The remaining synthesizers are used as slave synthesizers. In this lesson, you will not play the slave keyboards manually; instead, they will be controlled by the master keyboard (when you are recording a part) or by the sequencer (when you are playing back parts).

Step 3: Set the song tempo.
The music to be recorded in *Fig. 6.1* has a metronome marking of 80 *bpm* (beats per minute). Set your song tempo indicator to this value. If you can't play the music at the indicated tempo, choose a slower tempo for the recording process. Be sure to change

the tempo to the original value when you have finished recording. For example, if you feel more comfortable playing the parts at a metronome marking of 50 *bpm*, set the tempo indicator at 50 *bpm* and record the parts at this tempo. After you finish recording, change the tempo indicator to 80 *bpm*, and the sequencer will play back at the correct tempo.

Step 4: Set the time signature.
On most sequencers, you can enter the time signature by first locating the time signature on the sequencer screen and then entering the desired time signature. In this exercise, you would type "4" twice.

Step 5: Set the note (or record) resolution value to the highest resolution.
You will learn about sequencer resolution in Chapter 8. For now, set the resolution value to the highest resolution setting. This setting will give you the most accurate playback of your performance.

Step 6: Activate the metronome.
Since you will be overdubbing the remaining three parts of the sequence, you should use the metronome when recording each part. If your sequencer allows you to specify the number of clicks per measure, adjust the metronome so that it clicks 8 times per measure. Be sure that your synthesizer sound is soft enough so that you can hear the clicks at all times.

Step 7: Set the number of lead-in measures for the metronome.
A lead-in measure allows you to hear one measure of metronome clicks before the sequencer begins to record. On some sequencers, it is possible to vary the number of lead-in measures. A one measure lead-in should work well for this sequence.

Step 8: Assign the MIDI Channel number on Slave A to Channel 5.
In the setup chart (*Fig. 6.7*), you reserved MIDI Channel 5 for Slave A. The MIDI channel setting on most synthesizers is usually found in the "Utilities", "Global", or "MIDI" section of the instrument. (Consult your owner's manual to learn how to change the MIDI channel.)

Step 9: Change the MIDI channel number on the master keyboard to the channel number that is assigned to Slave A.
In the setup chart (*Fig. 6.7*), you decided to use Slave A to record the soprano part.

Since Slave A is assigned to MIDI Channel 5, you must also assign the master keyboard to transmit MIDI data to the sequencer on Channel 5.

Step 10: Assign Sequencer Track 1 to MIDI Channel 5.
Place the sequencer cursor on the line that designates the MIDI channel for Track 1 and set the channel number to 5.

Step 11: Activate the "MIDI ECHO" (sometimes called "MIDI THRU")
           function on the sequencer.
In Step 9 on this page, you changed the master keyboard's MIDI channel to Channel 5, the channel used by Slave A to play the soprano part. When MIDI ECHO is activated, the sequencer will send any incoming MIDI data through the sequencer MIDI OUT port. This means that the music you play on the master keyboard will be recorded by the sequencer and, at the same time, be passed to the MIDI OUT port which will send the data back to the master keyboard and to all slave synthesizers. Since the master keyboard is set to Channel 5, you will hear Slave A's flute sound when you play the master keyboard, and you will also hear a different sound from the master keyboard. To avoid this problem, see Step 12.

Step 12: Turn off the volume control for the master keyboard.
When you play the master keyboard, you will hear the sound of the flute (Slave A) and the sound from the master keyboard. In order to hear only the flute sound, simply turn off the volume control for the master keyboard and you will hear only the sound from Slave A.

Step 13: Assign the sound for the first track on the sequencer.
In the setup chart (*Fig. 6.7*), you selected the flute sound (Program 24 on Slave A) for the soprano part. Place the sequencer's cursor on the program number line for Track 1, and enter the number 24. At this point, the program number on the master keyboard might also switch to Program 24. Don't worry about this - remember, you're not hearing the master keyboard yet.

Step 14: Adjust the volume level of the sound.
Never record a sound at the maximum volume level because, when the need arises, it becomes impossible to make the sound louder. As a general rule, you should set the volume level at about 80% of maximum level so that you will be able to increase volume level when needed.

Step 15: Identify the contents of the first track with a name.

If your sequencer allows you to name an empty track, place the cursor on the *name line* for Track 1 and type the word "Soprano". Your sequencer screen should now look something like *Fig. 6.9*.

SONG NAME: Fortress		TIME SIG: 4/4
SONG TEMPO: 80 MIDI ECHO: Off		METRONOME: On

TRACK	NAME	MIDI CHANNEL	PROGRAM
1	Soprano	5	24
2		–	–
3		–	–
4		–	–
5		–	–
6		–	–
7		–	–
8		–	–

Fig. 6.9

Step 16: Record the first instrumental part of the multi-timbral sequence.

Now you are ready to record the first track of the sequence. See *Fig. 6.10*.

Fig. 6.10. The soprano part.

Before you begin, you must press the space bar or button labeled "Record", "REC" or START". While you are recording the soprano part, you will hear the sound of the metronome from the sequencer. The metronome is not being recorded.

Step 17: Assign the MIDI channel number on Slave B to Channel 6.

In the setup chart (*Fig. 6.7*), you reserved MIDI Channel 6 for Slave B.

78

Step 18: Change the MIDI channel on the master keyboard to the MIDI channel number assigned to the alto part (Slave B).

Change the master keyboard's MIDI channel to Channel 6 and play the alto part. You should hear only the oboe sound which you selected in the setup chart (*Fig. 6.7*).

Step 19: Select a different sequencer track for the second instrumental part.

In order to record the second part (alto part) using a different timbre, you must record the alto part on a different track. You selected Track 2. Refer to *Fig. 6.7*. On most sequencers, you can select a different track by placing the cursor on the line that designates the desired track. (Consult your owner's manual to learn how to record on different tracks.)

Step 20: Assign the second track of the sequencer to the same MIDI channel number used for the alto part (Slave B).

The alto part is assigned to MIDI Channel 6 on Slave B. Place the sequencer cursor on the line which designates the MIDI channel number for Track 2 and set the channel number to 6.

Step 21: Assign the sound for the second track on the sequencer.

In the setup chart (*Fig. 6.7*), you selected the oboe sound (Program 13) for the alto part. Place the sequencer's cursor on the program number line for Track 2 and enter the number 13.

Step 22: If possible, use the sequencer to adjust the volume level of the sounds.

Adjust the volume levels so that you have a balance between the flute sound on Track 1 and the oboe sound that you will be recording on Track 2.

Step 23: Identify the contents of the second track with a name.

If your sequencer allows you to name a track, place the cursor on the name line and type the word "Alto". The sequencer screen should now look something like Fig. *6.11*.

| SONG NAME: Fortress | | TIME SIG: 4/4 |
| SONG TEMPO: 80 | MIDI ECHO: Off | METRONOME: On |

TRACK	NAME	MIDI CHANNEL	PROGRAM
1	Soprano	5	24
2	Alto	6	13
3		–	–
4		–	–
5		–	–
6		–	–
7		–	–
8		–	–

Fig. 6.11

Step 24: Record the second instrumental part of the multi-timbral sequence.

At this point, you are ready to record the alto part. While you are recording on Track 2, you will hear the soprano part on Track 1 and the metronome. When you finish recording the alto part, you will have two musical parts recorded on two separate tracks. When you play back the sequence, you will hear the music in *Fig. 6.12*.

Fig. 6.12 Soprano and alto parts

Step 25: Assign the MIDI channel number on Slave C to Channel 7.

Channel 7 was reserved for Slave C. Refer to the setup chart in *Fig. 6.7*.

Step 26: Change the MIDI channel number on the master keyboard to the MIDI channel assigned to the tenor part (Slave C).

In the setup chart (*Fig. 6.7*), you assigned Slave C (clarinet) to MIDI Channel 7. When you change the master keyboard's MIDI channel to 7, you will hear only the clarinet sound.

Step 27: Select a different sequencer track for the third instrumental part.
In order to record the third part (tenor part) using a different timbre, you must record the tenor part on an empty track. In the setup chart (*Fig. 6.7*), you selected Track 3 for the tenor part.

Step 28: Assign the third track of the sequencer to the same MIDI channel
           used for the tenor part (Slave C).
The tenor part (clarinet sound) is assigned to MIDI Channel 7 on Slave C. Place the sequencer cursor on the line which designates the MIDI channel number for Track 3 and set the channel number to 7.

Step 29: Assign the sound for the third track on the sequencer.
In the setup chart (*Fig. 6.7*), you selected the clarinet sound (Program 47) for the tenor part. Place the sequencer's cursor on the program number line for Track 3 and enter the number 47.

Step 30: Adjust the volume level of the sounds.
If your sequencer has a volume level setting for each track, adjust the volume levels so that you have a balance between the flute sound on Track 1, the oboe sound on Track 2, and the clarinet sound you will be recording on Track 3.

Step 31: Identify the contents of the third track with a name.
Place the cursor on the name line for Track 3 and type the word "Tenor". Your sequencer screen should now look something like *Fig. 6.13*.

| SONG NAME: Fortress | | | TIME SIG: 4/4 |
| SONG TEMPO: 80 | MIDI ECHO: Off | | METRONOME: On |

TRACK	NAME	MIDI CHANNEL	PROGRAM
1	Soprano	5	24
2	Alto	6	13
3	Tenor	7	47
4		–	–
5		–	–
6		–	–
7		–	–
8		–	–

Fig. 6.13

Step 32: Record the third instrumental part of the multi-timbral sequence.
Now you are ready to record the tenor part. While you are recording on Track 3, you will hear the alto part on Track 2, the soprano part on Track 1, and the metronome. When you finish recording the tenor part, you will have three musical parts recorded on three separate tracks. When you play back the sequence, you should hear the music in *Fig. 6.14.*

Fig. 6.14 Soprano, alto and tenor parts

Step 33: Change the MIDI channel on the master keyboard to the MIDI channel assigned to the bass part.
Channel 8 was reserved for the master keyboard (bass part). Refer to the setup chart in *Fig. 6.7.*

Step 34: Turn off the "MIDI ECHO" or "MIDI THRU" function on the sequencer.
If MIDI THRU is activated, the sequencer will send any incoming MIDI data through the sequencer's MIDI OUT port. When you play the master keyboard, the synthesizer will play two identical notes whenever you play a note on the keyboard. The synthesizer's microprocessor (or "brain") receives a command to play a note from the keyboard and another command from the sequencer to play the same note. This doubling of every note changes the tone quality of certain sounds. It also reduces the number of notes that can be played simultaneously. Because you now want to use the master keyboard as a sound source and not just as a controller, turn off the MIDI THRU function on the sequencer.

Step 35: Turn up the volume of the master keyboard.
Because you are now using the master keyboard as a sound source for the bass part, turn up the volume to its normal level.

Step 36: Select a different sequencer track for the fourth musical part.
In order to record the bass part (bassoon) using a different timbre, you must record the bassoon part on any empty track. In the setup chart (*Fig. 6.7*), you selected Track 4 for the bass part.

Step 37: Assign the fourth track of the sequencer to the same MIDI channel used for the bass part.
In the setup chart (*Fig. 6.7*), you assigned the master keyboard to MIDI Channel 8 on the synthesizer. Place the sequencer cursor on the line which designates the MIDI channel for Track 4 and set the channel number to 8.

Step 38: Assign the sound for the fourth track on the sequencer.
In the setup chart (*Fig. 6.7*), you selected the bassoon sound (Program 11) for the bass part. Place the sequencer cursor on the program line for Track 4 and enter "11."

Step 39: Adjust the volume level of the sounds.
Adjust the volume levels so that you have a balance between the flute sound on Track 1, the oboe sound on Track 2, the clarinet sound on Track 3, and the bassoon sound you will be recording on Track 4.

Step 40: Identify the contents of the fourth track with a name.
Place the cursor on the name line for Track 4 and type the word "Bass". Your sequencer screen should now look something like *Fig. 6.15*.

SONG NAME: Fortress		TIME SIG: 4/4
SONG TEMPO: 80	MIDI ECHO: Off	METRONOME: On

TRACK	NAME	MIDI CHANNEL	PROGRAM
1	Soprano	5	24
2	Alto	6	13
3	Tenor	7	47
4	Bass	8	11
5		–	—
6		–	—
7		–	—
8		–	—

Fig. 6.15

Step 41: Record the fourth instrumental part of the multi-timbral sequence.
Now you are ready to record the bass part. While you are recording on Track 4, you will hear the tenor part on Track 3, the alto part on Track 2, the soprano part on Track 1, and the metronome. When you finish recording the bass part, you will have four musical parts recorded on four separate tracks. When you play back the sequence, you should hear the music in *Fig. 6.16.*

Fig. 6.16. Soprano, alto, tenor, and bass parts.

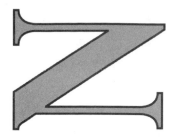
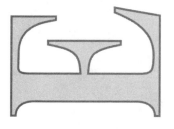
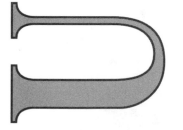

SECTION 3

BASIC EDITING TECHNIQUES

In Section 3, you will learn how to correct and how to enhance your music by using editing techniques. You can use editing techniques to do anything from correcting the pitch of one note to creating a totally new and different interpretation of your sequence. An understanding of editing techniques will enable you to create sequences which are technically correct and musical.

Chapter 7

HOW TO CORRECT WRONG NOTES

There are three techniques for correcting notes in a sequence track: **re-recording,** **punch-in,** and **event editing.** Let's examine each of these techniques in detail.

TECHNIQUE #1: CORRECTING NOTES BY RE-RECORDING

If a track contains many mistakes, it's sometimes easier to erase the track and to record the part again. If you continue to make the same mistakes in the same places, you should practice and master the troublesome passages before continuing to record, or you should record the part at a slower tempo.

TECHNIQUE #2: CORRECTING NOTES USING PUNCH-IN

Punch-in is a powerful feature that allows you to re-record any portion of a track without having to record the entire track. For many performers, punch-in is usually the fastest and easiest way to correct or to improve a track. Suppose that you want to record the music in *Fig. 7.1* on Track 1 of your sequencer..

Fig. 7.1

When you record the music, however, let's assume that you make two mistakes in Measure 7. See *Fig. 7.2*.

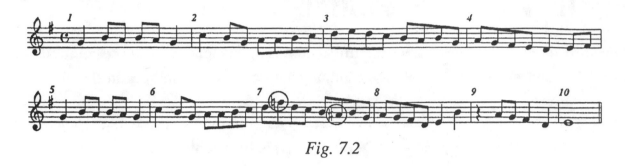

Fig. 7.2

To correct these notes using punch-in, follow the steps listed below.

Step 1: Make a backup copy of the original track.

Note: If your sequencer has an "Undo" function, skip this step.

Use the sequencer feature called "Track Copy" to make a backup copy of the original track. If you accidentally damage or erase the original track, you can use the backup copy. Be sure to mute the backup track.

Step 2: Identify the measure or measures that you want to re-record.
The starting point of the measure or notes that you want to re-record is called the **punch-in point.** The ending point is called the **punch-out point.** All of the music between these two points will be erased when you use punch-in. In *Fig. 7.2*, the punch-in point will be at the beginning of Measure 7, and the punch-out point will be at the end of Measure 7. On most sequencers, you would enter this information by placing the sequencer cursor on the "punch-in measure number line" and typing "7", and then by placing the cursor on the "punch-out number line" and typing "7" again.

> *Note: All sequencers do not have the same punch-in and punch-out capabilities. Some sequencers allow you to specify punch-in points and punch-out points at any location within a measure. Other sequencers allow you to specify punch-in points and punch-out points only at the beginning or at the end of a measure. If your sequencer uses only measure numbers for punch-in and punch-out points, check to see how your sequencer defines the punch-out point. On some sequencers, selecting a punch-out point at Measure 7 means that the sequencer will actually stop re-recording at the end of Measure 6. On other sequencers, a punch-out point at Measure 7 means that the sequencer will re-record through Measure 7 and will stop re-recording just before the beginning of Measure 8. Be sure you know which way your sequencer operates or you might accidentally erase one measure too many.*

Step 3: Set the number of lead-in measures.

The **lead-in measure number** determines how many measures of the sequence you will hear before the punch-in begins. Be sure to select a lead-in point that gives you enough time to prepare for the punch-in. For this example, select Measure 5 as the lead-in measure. On most sequencers this is done by placing the sequencer cursor on the lead-in measure value and entering the number "5".

Step 4: If you used a metronome when you originally recorded the track, activate the metronome before you record the punch-in.

Using the metronome will help in making your punch-in sound more consistent with the original recording and less likely to be detected.

Step 5: Be sure to select the correct track before you begin recording.

This step is very important when you are working with multi-track sequences. In this example, you would select Track 1.

Step 6: Record the punch-in.

The following recording procedures will help you produce a good punch-in.

Recording Procedure #1: When recording the punch-in, start playing along with the music before the punch-in point, and continue to play after the punch-out point.

One of the audible signs of a punch-in is a sudden change in the phrasing of a musical line. Playing the part a little before the punch-in point and a little after the punch-out point will often make the punch-in less obvious by maintaining the flow of the musical line. In this example, start playing the music in Measure 6, even though your playing will not be recorded until Measure 7. When you get to Measure 7, the sequencer will automatically begin to record. You should play through Measure 7 and into Measure 8, even though the sequencer will automatically stop recording at the end of Measure 7. This technique of playing through the punch points helps to ensure a natural flow of music.

Recording Procedure #2: Match the dynamics of the punch-in music with the rest of the musical line.

Another audible sign of a punch-in is a sudden change in dynamics in the middle of a musical phrase. When you re-record Measure 7, be sure to match the dynamic level of the new musical material with the rest of the phrase.

Recording Procedure #3: For difficult music, slow down the tempo to record the punch-in.

Remember, a change in the song tempo will not affect pitch. You can record the punch-in music at a slow tempo, and then have the sequencer play back the music at the correct tempo.

After you have recorded your punch-in, listen to the entire phrase very carefully. A good punch-in is inaudible. If your punch-in doesn't sound right, try to analyze what is wrong. Remember, the obvious signs of a punch-in are sudden differences in dynamics or phrasing. Once you have identified the problem, try to correct the error by punching in again.

Step 7: Insert missing notes if they occur.

The occasional disappearance of a note in the first measure after a punch-out is a problem that may occur from time to time. For example, let's suppose that you made a seemingly perfect punch-in on Measure 7 in *Fig. 7.2*. When you play the part back, however, you hear the music shown in *Fig. 7.3*.

Fig. 7.3

The note "A" on the first beat of Measure 8 vanished because it was inadvertently played at the end of Measure 7. This is a common occurrence with performers who play slightly ahead of the beat, especially when the tempo is fast or the music is technically demanding. You may have thought that you played the note "A" on the first beat of Measure 8, but the sequencer recorded the note as if it were the last note of Measure 7.

There are two ways to restore the disappearing note. The first way is simply to extend the punch-out point to the end of Measure 8. Since Measure 9 begins with a rest on the first beat, there is no danger of erasing any notes on the first beat of Measure 9. The second way to restore the disappearing note is to use another editing technique called event editing. A detailed explanation of event editing will follow in TECHNIQUE #3, **CORRECTING NOTES USING EVENT EDITING** (p.91).

Step 8: If you made a backup copy of the original track in Step 1, erase the backup track.

To avoid possible confusion, erase the backup track as soon as all corrections have been made.

TECHNIQUE #3: CORRECTING NOTES USING EVENT EDITING

In Chapter 2 you learned that sequencers record MIDI data, not acoustical sounds. MIDI data is information that digitally represents a note's *pitch* (the specific key that was struck), *velocity level* (the speed with which the key was struck), *starting time* (the exact moment when the key was struck), and *duration* (the length of time the key was held down). Event editing makes it possible to alter this information as well as other types of MIDI data. In Part 1 below, you will learn how to read note names in a **MIDI event list**. In Part 2, you will learn how to use event editing to correct wrong notes.

PART 1 - READING NOTE NAMES IN A MIDI EVENT LIST

Suppose that you record the C major scale in *Fig. 7.4* on Track 1 of your sequencer precisely as written. The sequencer records the performance not as acoustical sound but as digital information that describes or represents the performance. The sequencer stores this information in memory.

You can access this information and view it on your display. By using the cursor to change the numerical information, you can change various aspects of the performance. To accomplish this you must access the MIDI event list. On most sequencers, this is a two step process. First, find the menu prompt which reads something like "EVENT EDIT", "EVENT LISTING" or "MIDI EVENT LIST". Next, specify the specific sequencer track that you would like to view as an event list.

Although the physical appearance of MIDI event lists can vary greatly from one sequencer screen to another, the MIDI data contained in these lists is the same. *Fig. 7.5* is an example of a typical MIDI event list.

Fig. 7.4

The list below represents the performance of the C major scale in *Fig. 7.4*. Let's examine this list more closely.

A	B	C	D	E	F
Measure #	Event #	Event Type	Start Time	Duration	Velocity
1	1	C3	1:00	0:95	87
1	2	D3	2:00	0:95	87
1	3	E3	3:00	1:47	89
1	4	F3	4:48	0:47	80
2	1	G3	1:00	0:95	36
2	2	A3	2:00	0:47	80
2	3	B3	2:48	0:47	81
2	4	C4	3:00	1:95	86
2	5	G3	3:00	1:95	86
2	6	E3	3:00	1:95	90

Fig. 7.5. A MIDI event list for the music in Fig. 7.4.

Column A displays the measure number of the sequence. The music in *Fig. 7.4* contains only two measures; therefore, the display shows the events in Measure 1 and Measure 2.

Column B displays the event number in the measure. The event number shows the chronological placement of events in each measure. Measure 1 of *Fig. 7.4* contains four notes - C,D,E, and F. Each note is considered an event; therefore, in *Fig. 7.5*, the event list for Measure 1 contains four events listed in chronological order. Measure 2 in *Fig. 7.4* contains six notes, so the event list for Measure 2 contains six events. The final chord in Measure 2 is not one event; chords are made up of individual notes, and each note is a separate event.

Column C displays the event type for each event in a measure. In the first event of Measure 1 in *Fig. 7.5*, "C3" is displayed under the Event Type column. "C" indicates the note; "3" indicates the octave in which the note was played. MIDI can send and receive note data over a ten octave range, from C-2 (five octaves below middle C on a piano), to G8 (more than five octaves above middle C). The octaves are identified from lowest to highest as follows: -2, -1, 0, 1, 2, 3, 4, 5, 6, 7, 8. See *Fig. 7.6*.

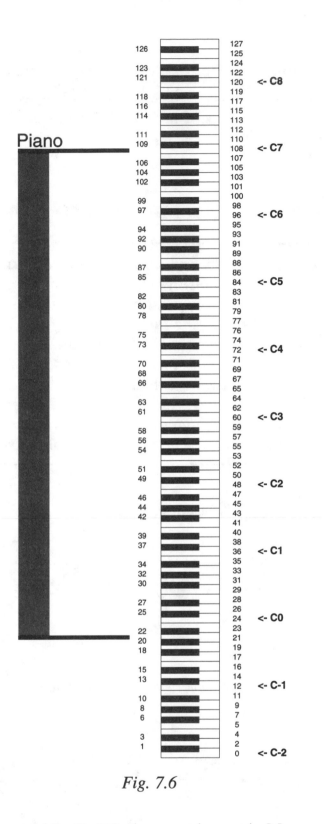

Fig. 7.6

In *Fig. 7.6,* C3 represents middle C. D3, the second event in Measure 1, represents the D two semitones higher than C3. The higher the number after the note name, the higher the note's octave. The lower the number after the note name, the lower the note's octave.

(**Column D** and **Column E** in *Fig. 7.5* display the event starting time and the event duration, or length. These variables will be described in detail in Chapter 8. **Column F** displays the note velocity - the speed in which each key on the keyboard was struck. Velocity editing will be described in Chapter 9.)

PART 2 - USING EVENT EDITING TO CORRECT NOTES

> *Note: Many synthesizers include keyboards that are both velocity sensitive and pressure sensitive. A pressure sensitive keyboard enables you to change one or more aspects of a sound by applying pressure to a key that is already depressed. If you use pressure on some keys during the recording of the following exercise, you will generate additional MIDI data and will therefore have many more events in your event list. For the purpose of simplifying, therefore, disengage the pressure sensitivity control for the following exercise. On most instruments, this can be accomplished by entering the "GLOBAL" or "UTILITIES" section of the instrument and by locating the master setting that usually reads "Aftertouch ON/OFF" or "AFT DISABLE/ENABLE". Aftertouch is another term for pressure sensitivity.*

Suppose that you want to record the melody in *Fig. 7.7* on Track 1 of your sequencer.

Fig. 7.7

When you record the melody, however, you play the three wrong notes as shown in *Fig. 7.8*.

Fig. 7.8

To correct the notes using event editing, follow the steps listed below.

Step 1: Make a backup copy of the original track.

Note: If your sequencer has an "Undo" function, skip this step.

Use the sequencer feature called "Track Copy" to make a backup copy of the original track. If you accidentally damage or erase the original track, you can use the backup copy. Be sure to mute the backup track.

Step 2: Identify the track and measure numbers containing the wrong notes.

Before you enter the event editing mode, be sure you know the track and the measure number that contains the wrong notes. You can usually read the measure numbers on the sequencer display while the sequence is being played back. In this example, Measures 2, 3, and 5 contain wrong notes.

Step 3: Access the MIDI event list for the track containing the wrong notes.

On most sequencers, this is a two step process. First, find the menu prompt which reads something like "EVENT EDIT", "EVENT LISTING" or "MIDI EVENT LIST". Next, specify the sequencer track you would like to view as an event list. In this example, you would specify Track 1. Your event list for the music in *Fig. 7.8* should look something like *Fig 7.9.* on the next page.

Step 4: Locate the first measure containing a wrong note in the event list.

On most sequencers, you would place the cursor in **Column A (Measure #)** and step through the measures by pressing the "+" button or "value up" key. In this example, locate Measure 2.

Step 5: Locate the wrong note in the measure.

On most sequencers, you place the cursor in **Column C (Event Type)** and step through each note in the measure until you come to the wrong note. In this example, the first wrong note is C3 (Event #8 in Measure 2).

95

A Measure #	B Event #	C Event Type	D Start Time	E Duration	F Velocity
1	1	C3	1:00	0:95	76
1	2	C4	2:00	0:95	87
1	3	B3	3:00	0:47	80
1	4	A3	3:48	0:47	82
1	5	G3	4:00	0:95	76
2	1	A3	1:00	0:47	82
2	2	C3	1:48	0:47	84
2	3	G3	2:00	0:47	86
2	4	C3	2:48	0:47	83
2	5	F3	3:00	0:47	80
2	6	A3	3:48	0:47	82
2	7	G3	4:00	0:47	79
2	8	C3	4:48	0:47	90
3	1	D3	1:00	0:95	91
3	2	C4	2:00	0:95	87
3	3	D4	3:00	0:47	90
3	4	B3	3:48	0:47	83
3	5	G3	4:00	0:95	88
4	1	A3	1:00	0:47	86
4	2	C3	1:48	0:47	90
4	3	G3	2:00	0:47	90
4	4	C3	2:48	0:47	88
4	5	F3	3:00	0:47	93
4	6	A3	3:48	0:47	82
4	7	D4	4:00	0:47	92
4	8	G3	4:48	0:47	87
5	1	D4	1:00	0:05	88
5	2	E4	1:00	3.95	97

Fig. 7.9 This is an event list for the music in Fig. 7.8.

Step 6: Correct the pitch of the wrong note.

To change the pitch of the C3, you place the cursor on the "C3" in the list, and then press the minus key (-) or the "value down" key once to change the "C3" to "B2". You don't have to change anything else or play anything on the keyboard. You haven't changed the note's starting time, duration, or dynamic level. Everything about the note will remain the same, except for the note's pitch.

Step 7: Listen to the correction.

Verify your edit by listening to the sequence.

The second wrong note in *Fig. 7.8* is the note "D" on the first beat of the third measure. Refer to Steps 1-5 and make the correction yourself. If you can't, follow the steps in the next paragraph.

To correct this mistake, do the following:

- Locate Measure 3 in **Column A** of *Fig. 7.9*.
- Locate the wrong note in Measure 3. The note D3 (Event #1) should have been recorded as C3.
- Correct the mistake by changing the D3 in the list to C3, using the technique described in Step 5 above.

The final mistake in the musical example is in Measure 5 of *Fig. 7.8*. This type of mistake is called a "smudge" - an accidental sounding of two keys on the keyboard. The smudge note in this example is D4. Most sequencers allow you to remove or to delete an event. To delete the D4 from the music, do the following:

- Locate Measure 5 in the event list in *Fig. 7.9*.
- Locate the event number in Measure 5 that contains D4. In *Fig. 7.9*, the D4 in Measure 5 is listed as Event #1.
- Correct the mistake by deleting Event #1 from the event list. On most sequencers this is accomplished by pressing a button labeled "erase" or "delete". (Consult your sequencer manual to learn how to delete an event.) When you delete event #1, all remaining events in the measure are re-numbered. Event #2 now becomes Event #1, Event #3 now becomes Event #2, and so on.

Step 8: If you made a backup copy of the original track in Step 1, erase the backup track.

To avoid possible confusion, erase the backup track as soon as all corrections have been made.

If you use a word processor, you will realize that correcting a misspelled word is very much like correcting a wrong note. You find the misspelled word; move the cursor to the misspelled word; and correct the word by typing in the correct spelling or by deleting characters. The computer is a word processor that works with digital data representing words. A sequencer is a music processor that works with digital data representing music. Word processing and music processing have much in common; try to apply the principles from one area to another.

Re-recording, punch-in, and event edit - these are the most common methods of correcting wrong notes. In the next chapter, you will learn how to use these methods to correct rhythms.

Chapter 8

HOW TO CORRECT RHYTHMIC ERRORS

There are four techniques for correcting rhythms in a sequence: **re-recording, punch-in, event edit, and quantization.** Let's examine each of these methods in detail.

TECHNIQUE #1: CORRECTING RHYTHMS BY RE-RECORDING

If a track contains many mistakes, it's sometimes easier to erase the track and to record the part again. If you continue to make the same mistakes in the same places, you should practice and master the troublesome passage before continuing to record, or you should record the part at a slower tempo.

TECHNIQUE #2: CORRECTING RHYTHMS USING PUNCH-IN

Punch-in is a powerful feature that allows you to re-record any portion of a track without having to record the entire track. For many performers, punch-in is usually the fastest and easiest way to correct or to improve a track.

Let's suppose that you want to record the music in *Fig. 8.1* on Track 1 of your sequencer.

Fig. 8.1

When you record the part, however, you make rhythmic errors in Measure 6 as shown in *Fig. 8.2*.

Fig. 8.2

To correct these rhythmic errors using punch-in, follow the steps listed below.

Step 1: Make a backup copy of the original track.

Note: If your sequencer has an "Undo" function, skip this step.

Use the sequencer feature called "Track Copy" to make a backup copy of the original track. If you accidentally damage or erase the original track, you can use the backup copy.

Step 2: Identify the measure or measures that you want to re-record.
The starting point of the measure or notes that you want to re-record is called the **punch-in point.** The ending point is called the **punch-out point.** All of the music between these two points will be erased when you use punch-in. In *Fig. 8.2*, the punch-in point will be at the beginning of Measure 6, and the punch-out point will be at the end of Measure 6. On most sequencers, you would enter this information by placing the sequencer cursor on the "punch-in measure number line" and typing "6", and then by placing the cursor on the "punch-out number line" and typing "6" again.

Note: All sequencers do not have the same punch-in and punch-out capabilities. Some sequencers allow you to specify punch-in points and punch-out points at any location within a measure. Other sequencers allow you to specify punch-in points and punch-out points only at the beginning or at the end of a measure. If your sequencer uses only measure numbers for punch-in and punch-out points, check to see how your sequencer defines the punch-out point. On some sequencers, selecting a punch-out point at Measure 7 means that the sequencer will actually stop re-recording at the end of Measure 6. On other sequencers, a punch-out point at Measure 7 means that the sequencer will re-record through Measure 7 and will stop re-recording just before the beginning of Measure 8. Be sure you know which way your sequencer operates, or you might accidentally erase one measure too many.

Step 3: Set the number of lead-in measures.

The lead-in measure number determines how many measures of the sequence you will hear before the punch-in begins. Be sure to select a lead-in point that gives you enough time to prepare for the punch-in. For this example, select Measure 4 as the lead-in measure. On most sequencers this is done by placing the sequencer cursor on the lead-in measure value and entering the number "4".

Step 4: If you used a metronome when you originally recorded a track, activate the metronome before you record the punch-in.

Using the metronome will help in making your punch-in sound more consistent with the original recording and less likely to be detected.

Step 5: Be sure to select the correct track before you begin recording.

This step is very important when you are working with multi-track sequences. In this example you would select Track 1.

Step 6: Record the punch-in.

The following recording procedures will help you produce a good punch-in.

> **Recording Procedure #1: When recording the punch-in, start playing along with the music before the punch-in point, and continue to play after the punch-out point.**
>
> One of the audible signs of a punch-in is a sudden change in the phrasing of a musical line. Playing the part a little before the punch-in point and a little after the punch-out point will often make the punch-in less obvious by maintaining the flow of the entire musical line. In this example, start playing the music in Measure 5, even though your playing will not be recorded until Measure 6. When you get to Measure 6, the sequencer will automatically begin to record. You should play through Measure 6 and into Measure 7, even though the sequencer will automatically stop recording at the end of Measure 6. This technique of playing through the punch points helps to ensure a natural flow of music.
>
> **Recording Procedure #2: Match the dynamics of the punch-in music with the rest of the musical line.**
>
> Another audible sign of a punch-in is a sudden change in dynamics in the middle of a musical phrase. When you re-record Measure 6, be sure to match the dynamic level of the new musical material with the rest of the phrase.

Recording Procedure #3: **For difficult music, slow down the song tempo to record the punch-in.**

Remember, a change in the song tempo will not affect pitch. You can record the punch-in music at a slow tempo, and then have the sequencer play back the music at a faster tempo.

After you have recorded your punch-in, listen to the entire phrase very carefully. A good punch-in is inaudible. If your punch-in doesn't sound right, try to analyze what is wrong. Remember, the obvious signs of a punch-in are sudden differences in dynamics or phrasing. Once you have identified the problem, try to correct the error by punching in again.

Step 7: Insert missing notes if they occur.
Review Step 7 on p.90, if necessary.

Step 8: If you made a backup copy of the original track in Step 1, erase the backup track.
To avoid possible confusion, erase the backup track as soon as all corrections have been made.

TECHNIQUE #3: CORRECTING RHYTHMS USING EVENT EDITING

In Chapter 7, you learned how to use event editing to correct notes. In this chapter, you will learn how to use event editing to correct rhythms. In Part 1 of this section, you will learn how rhythms are represented in a MIDI event list. In Part 2, you will learn how to use event editing to correct rhythms.

PART 1 - READING NOTE RHYTHMS IN A MIDI EVENT LIST

Suppose that you played along with the metronome and recorded the following melody on Track 1 of your sequencer.

Fig. 8.3

If you play each note with 100% rhythmic accuracy, the event list display will appear as in *Fig. 8.4*.

A Measure #	B Event #	C Event Type	D Start Time	E Duration	F Velocity
1	1	G3	1:00	0:95	92
1	2	G3	2:00	0:47	84
1	3	D4	3:00	0:95	91
1	4	D4	4:00	0:47	87
2	1	C4	1:00	1:47	92
2	2	B3	2:48	0:47	86
2	3	A3	3:00	0:95	90
3	1	G3	1:00	1:95	92

Fig. 8.4 The MIDI event list for the music in Fig. 8.3.

In Chapter 7, you learned the following:
- **Column A** displays the measure numbers of the sequence. (You can see that this sequence has only 3 measures.)
- **Column B** displays the number of events in each measure. (Measure 1 has 4 events; Measure 2 has 3 events; Measure 3 has 1 event.)
- **Column C** displays the type of event. (In this example, you are working only with note events.)
- **Column D** displays the starting time for each event. (Every event in this event list starts on the beat except Event 2 in Measure 2. Explanation will follow).
- **Column E** displays the event duration or the time value for each note. (Explanation will follow.)
- **Column F** displays the speed with which each key was struck. (Velocity editing will be explained in Chapter 9.)

The information displayed in **Columns A, B**, and **C** should not be a problem at this point; however, **Columns D** and **E** need a more detailed explanation. First, you need to know about sequencer resolution.

Sequencer **resolution** refers to the sequencer's ability to divide the beat of a quarter note into a number of equal pulses. The higher a sequencer's resolution, the more accurately the sequencer can record and play back music. Sequencer resolution is measured in **pulses per quarter note**, which is usually abbreviated as *ppqn* or *ppq*. Older sequencers were capable of dividing a quarter note into only 24 equal parts. In other words, the sequencer resolution was 24 *ppqn*. More powerful sequencers can divide the quarter note into 48 parts (48 *ppqn*), 96 parts (96 *ppqn*), and 192 parts (192 *ppqn*). A few sequencers have even higher resolutions.

Let's assume that you are using a sequencer with a resolution of 96 pulses per quarter note. If you look at *Fig. 8.5*, you will see a Sequencer Resolution Chart.

NOTE VALUE to PULSE VALUE FOR 96 PPQN SEQUENCERS	
whole note	384 pulses
half note	192 pulses
triplet half note	128 pulses
quarter note	96 pulses
triplet quarter note	64 pulses
eighth note	48 pulses
triplet eighth note	32 pulses
sixteenth note	24 pulses
triplet sixteenth note	16 pulses
thirty-second note	12 pulses
triplet thirty-second note	8 pulses
sixty-fourth note	6 pulses
triplet sixty-fourth note	4 pulses

Fig. 8.5 Sequencer Resolution Chart

In the left hand column, you will find a list of note names placed in descending order of time value. Opposite each note name you will find a *ppqn* number. Remember, in this lesson your sequencer has a resolution of 96 *ppqn*; therefore, the *ppqn* number opposite the quarter note is 96. All other pulse numbers in this list are multiples or divisions of the *ppqn* number. If a quarter note has a *ppqn* resolution of 96, an eighth note has a *ppqn* resolution of 48, a sixteenth note has a *ppqn* resolution of 24, and so on. Refer to this chart whenever necessary.

Look at the music in the first measure of *Fig. 8.3*. Now look at **Column D** in the MIDI event list in *Fig. 8.4*. You can see that the start time for the first note (G3) is represented by the numbers "1:00". The number to the left of the colon represents the beat within a measure. Since the musical example in *Fig. 8.3* contains four beats in each measure, the number to the left of the colon will represent beat 1, beat 2, beat 3, or beat 4.

The two digits to the right of the colon in **Column D** represent subdivisions of the quarter note. Look at *Fig. 8.4*. In Measure 1, the first event is the note G3 and it starts on beat 1. Event 2 starts on beat 2. Now, look at Measure 2, Event 2. Notice that the start time for the note B3 is 2:48. This means that the note B starts 48 pulses after the second beat in the measure. If you look at the Sequencer Resolution Chart (*Fig. 8.5*) you will see that 48 pulses represent an eighth note. Therefore, you must conclude that the note B in Measure 2 begins on the second half of beat 2. If you look at all of the entries in **Column D**, you can draw the following conclusions:

- When the "Start Time" beat number is followed by a colon and two zeros (1:00, 2:00, etc.) it means that a note begins exactly on the beat.
- When the "Start Time" beat number is followed by a colon and additional numbers (1:48, 2:24, etc.), it means that a note begins at some point after the beat.

Now you are ready to decipher the information in **Column E - Duration**. **Column E** can not exist without **Column D**. Every note event must have a beginning and an end. Look at *Fig. 8.4*, and observe that the duration numbers resemble the START TIME numbers; however, they are different. The digit to the left of the colon represents a note's duration in terms of quarter notes. The digits to the right of the colon represent a note's duration measured in terms of subdivisions of a quarter note.

For example, if you look at a digital watch, you will notice that time is represented in terms of hours and minutes. Suppose that you look at the watch and it reads 03:54. You wait 10 minutes and look again. It does not read 03:64; instead, it reads 04:04. Whenever the minute dial reaches 00:59, it completes a cycle. It prepares to advance the hour dial forward and to reset the minute dial to 00:00. The duration time of a sequencer works in a similar manner, except that the sequencer in this example uses 96 pulses as a reference instead of 60 minutes. Whenever the sequencer pulse count reaches 95 it completes a cycle. On the next pulse, it advances the digit on the left of the colon by one and resets the remaining digits to zeros. See *Fig. 8.6*.

```
CHRONOLOGICAL DURATION PULSE COUNT
AT A RESOLUTION OF 96 PPQN
              0:90
              0:91
              0:92
              0:93
              0:94
              0:95    Cycle complete; must be reset
              1:00    Reset
              1:01
              1:02
```

Fig. 8.6

The start time pulse actually starts on 0:00 of the duration, which is why the duration seems to end on pulse 95. If you look at the first event in *Fig. 8.4*, you will see that the duration for the note G3 (Measure 1, Event 1) is represented by the number 0:95. This means that total duration is 96 pulses - one pulse for the start time, and 95 pulses for the duration. To determine the duration of a note, always add 1 pulse count to the digits on the right of the colon.

Look at the second event in Measure 1 of *Fig. 8.4*. The start time for the second G3 is 2:00, which is the first ninety-sixth pulse of beat 2. The duration for G3 is 0:47. This means that the total duration for this note is 48 ninety-sixths. Since 96 pulses equal a quarter note on your sequencer, 48 pulses would equal one half a quarter note, or an eighth note. If you look at the music in *Fig. 8.3*, you can see that the second note in Measure 1 is indeed an eighth note.

Let's look at one more example. In *Fig. 8.3*,, the first note of the second measure is a dotted quarter note. If you look in *Fig. 8.4*, you can find this note listed as the first event in Measure 2 (C4). **Column D** displays the note start time as "1:00". **Column E** displays the note duration as "1:47". This means that the note is held 1 beat ("1:--"), plus 48 ninety-sixths of a beat (":47"), which equals half a beat. Therefore, the duration for this note equals one and one-half beats.

Let's review what you've learned.
- Sequencers use the quarter note as a reference for determining resolution capabilities.
- The higher the resolution, the greater the number of **pulses per quarter note**, and the greater the timing accuracy of the sequencer.
- Some sequencers use 24 *ppqn*, others use 48 *ppqn*, others use 96 *ppqn*, 192 *ppqn* or more.
- Many current sequencers have a resolution of 96 *ppqn*. If 96 *ppqn* equal a quarter note, then 48 pulses equal an eighth note, 24 pulses equal a sixteenth note, 12 pulses equal a 32nd note, and so on.

PART 2 - USING EVENT EDITING TO CORRECT RHYTHMS

Listed below is the step-by step procedure for correcting rhythms using event editing.

Step 1: Make a backup copy of the original track.

> *Note: If your sequencer has an "Undo" function, skip this step.*

Use the sequencer feature called "Track Copy" to make a backup of the original track. If you accidentally damage or erase the original track, you can use the backup copy. Be sure to mute the backup track.

Step 2: Identify the track and the measure number containing the rhythm you want to correct.

Before you enter the event editing mode, be sure you know the track and the measure number which contains the wrong rhythm. You can usually read the measure numbers on the sequencer display while the sequence is being played back.

Step 3: Access the MIDI event list for the track containing the wrong rhythm.

On most sequencers this is a two step process. First, find the menu prompt which reads something like "EVENT EDIT", "EVENT LISTING", or "MIDI EVENT LIST". Next, specify the sequencer track you would like to view as a MIDI event list.

Step 4: Locate the measure containing the wrong rhythm in the event list.

On most sequencers you would place the cursor in the "Measure #" column and step through the measures by pressing the "+" button or "value up" key.

Step 5: Locate the note with the wrong rhythm in the event list.

On most sequencers you would place the cursor in the "Event Type" column and step through each note in the measure until you come to the desired note.

Step 6: To correct the note's rhythm, change the note start time and/or the note duration.

There are four methods for altering a note's rhythm using event editing:

1: Moving A Note's Starting Point Back In Time.

2: Moving A Note's Starting Point Forward In Time.

3: Shortening A Note's Duration.

4: Lengthening A Note's Duration.

Let's examine these methods one at a time.

Method #1: Moving A Note's Starting Point Back In Time.

Let's take another look at the melody we've been using in this chapter.

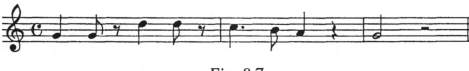

Fig. 8.7

Let's suppose that, after you record the melody into a sequencer, you want to change the rhythm in Measure 2 so that the melody will sound like this:

Fig. 8.8

This change can be made by editing the starting time of the note A3 (Measure 2, Event #3). See the event list in *Fig. 8.9*.

A Measure #	B Event #	C Event Type	D Start Time	E Duration	F Velocity
1	1	G3	1:00	00:95	92
1	2	G3	2:00	00:47	84
1	3	D4	3:00	00:95	91
1	4	D4	4:00	00:47	87
2	1	C4	1:00	01:47	92
2	2	B3	2:48	00:47	86
2	3	A3	3:00	00:95	90
3	1	G3	1:00	01:95	92

Fig. 8.9 The MIDI event list for the music in Fig. 8.7.

The event list in *Fig. 8.9* lists the starting time for this note as "3:00". By changing this value to "4:00", the note A will still be a quarter note, but it will now sound at the beginning of beat 4 as shown in *Fig. 8.8*. On most sequencers, you can change the note start time by first placing the cursor on the current start time value and then typing in the new value on a keypad.

Method #2:   Moving A Note's Starting Point Forward In Time.
Suppose that you want to change Measure 2 in *Fig. 8.8* so that it becomes like Measure 2 in *Fig. 8.10*.

Fig. 8.10

This change can be made by editing the starting time of the note B3 (Measure 2, Event 2). The event list in *Fig. 8.9* lists the note start time for B3 in Measure 2 as 2:48, which is the second half of beat two. By changing the note start time to 2:00, the note B will start at the beginning of beat 2. When you make this change and play back the sequence, however, you will hear the music as depicted in *Fig. 8.11*.

Fig. 8.11

The second beat of Measure 2 sounds like a mistake, because you hear the note C sustaining while the note B is played. C4, the first event of Measure 2, has a duration time of 1:47 pulses, which translates into one and a half beats. This explains why you still hear the note C when the note B is played. In order to correct this, you must use the next technique for changing a note's rhythm.

Method # 3: Shortening A Note's Duration.

You can correct the second beat of Measure 2 in *Fig. 8.11* by changing the duration of the note C4 (Measure 2, Event 1). The event list in *Fig. 8.9* lists the duration for C4 in Measure 2 as 1:47. By changing this value to 0:95, the note C4 will play for exactly one beat instead of one and one half beats. When you make this change and play back the sequence, you will hear the music in Measure 2 as shown in *Fig. 8.10*.

Method #4: Lengthening A Note's Duration.

Let's make one final change to our melody. Look at the music in *Fig. 8.10*. Suppose that you want to change the note B in Measure 2 from an eighth note into a half note, like this.

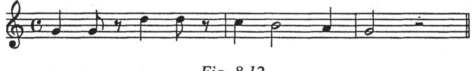

Fig. 8.12

This change can be made by lengthening the duration of the note. The event list in *Fig. 8.9* lists the duration for B3 in Measure 2 as 0:47 pulses, which equals one half beat. By changing this duration time to 1:95, the note B3 will now be sustained for exactly two beats. When you make this change and play back the sequence, you will hear the music shown in *Fig. 8.12*.

The examples in this section have shown how to change a note's starting time and duration by a full beat or by half a beat. By working with smaller changes in the note start time and duration, you can alter the phrasing and the feel of a musical line.

Step 7: Listen to the correction.
Verify your edit by listening to the track.

Step 8: If you made a backup copy of the original track in Step 1, erase the backup track.
To avoid possible confusion, erase the backup track as soon as all corrections have been made.

When you look at the note start times and durations on your event lists, don't expect to find exact start times and durations for your notes. At a resolution of 96 pulses per quarter note, it is impossible for anyone to record music into a sequencer and to have every note 100% rhythmically accurate. The note start times and durations listed in this chapter were precise so that you could better understand the mathematics involved in changing a note's rhythm.

TECHNIQUE #4: CORRECTING RHYTHMS USING QUANTIZATION

In Part 1 of this section, you will learn about quantization. In Part 2, you will learn how to correct rhythms using quantization.

PART 1 - UNDERSTANDING QUANTIZATION

Rhythmic **quantization** (sometimes called **autocorrect**) is the process of adjusting timing inaccuracies to a specific time value such as a quarter, eighth, sixteenth or thirty second note. In most cases, quantization is used to move note start times to the nearest beat or to the nearest subdivision of a beat.

For example, suppose that you record the scale in *Fig. 8.13* into the sequencer by playing along with the metronome.

Fig. 8.13

Fig. 8.14 is a MIDI event list for the music in *Fig. 8.13*. This list uses a sequencer resolution of 96 *ppqn*. For the purpose of illustration, let's suppose that **Columns D** and **E** represent your actual rhythmic performance.

A Measure #	B Event #	C Event Type	D Start Time	E Duration	F Velocity
1	1	C3	1:04	1:00	97
1	2	D3	2:03	1:03	98
1	3	E3	3:06	1:01	88
1	4	F3	4:01	0:94	87
2	1	G3	1:02	0:90	97
2	2	A3	1:94	0:94	99
2	3	B3	2:82	1:23	95
2	4	C4	4:10	0:85	89

Fig. 8.14

If you now quantize the scale to the nearest quarter note, the note start times would be moved to the exact starting point of each beat. *Fig. 8.15* shows the note start times of the quantized track.

A Measure #	B Event #	C Event Type	D Start Time	E Duration	F Velocity
1	1	C3	1:00	1:00	97
1	2	D3	2:00	1:03	98
1	3	E3	3:00	1:01	88
1	4	F3	4:00	0:94	87
2	1	G3	1:00	0:90	97
2	2	A3	3:00	1:23	95
2	3	B4	3:00	0:85	89
2	4	C4	4:00	0:85	89

Fig. 8.15

Now let's suppose you record another C Major scale into the sequencer by playing along with the metronome. This time, however, you played eighth notes instead of quarter notes. See *Fig. 8.16.*

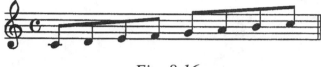

Fig. 8.16

Let's also suppose that you rush the tempo when you record the scale. *Fig. 8.17* is a MIDI event list of the music in *Fig. 8.16* as you performed it.

A Measure #	B Event #	C Event Type	D Start Time	E Duration	F Velocity
1	1	C3	1:04	0:42	97
1	3	E3	1:90	0:38	88
1	4	F3	2:37	0:46	87
1	5	G3	2:83	0:44	97
1	6	A3	3:34	0:46	99
1	7	B3	3:72	0:41	95
1	8	C3	4:20	0:42	89

Fig. 8.17

If you had played with 100% rhythmic accuracy, the note start times in **Column D** would have read as follows:

C Event Type	D Start Time
C3	1:00
D3	1:48
E3	2:00
F3	2:48
G3	3:00
A3	3:48
B3	4:00
C4	4:48

Fig. 8.18

By looking at the note start times in (**Column D**) in *Fig. 8.17*, you can see how the tempo rushed. If you quantize the note start time in *Fig. 8.17* to the nearest eighth beat, the following note start times would be created:

C Event Type	D Start Time
C3	1:00
D3	1:48
E3	2:00
F3	2:48
G3	3:00
A3	3:48
B3	4:00
C4	4:00

Fig. 8.19

Now If you play the sequence, you will hear the music in *Fig. 8.20*.

Fig. 8.20

What happened to the last note? If you look at the event list in *Fig. 8.17,* you will see that the start time for C4 was moved to 4:00 instead of 4:48. This occurred because the note was closer to the first half of beat four than it was to the second half of beat four. In *Fig. 8.17*, the unquantized start time for C4 was 4:20. In this example, an eighth note equals 48 clock pulses. Since 4:20 is closer to 4:00 than it is to 4:47, the note start time was moved to 4:00. (Remember, quantization moves notes to the nearest beat or subdivision of the beat.) For quantization to work properly, therefore, you have to play with some degree of accuracy.

PART 2 - USING QUANTIZATION TO CORRECT RHYTHMS

To correct rhythms using quantization, follow the steps listed below:

Step 1: Make a backup copy of the original track.

> *Note: If your sequencer has an "Undo" function, skip this step.*

Use the sequencer feature called "Track Copy" to make a backup copy of the original track. Be sure to mute the backup track.

Step 2: Identify the desired track and measure number(s) to be quantized.
Be sure you know the track and the measure number(s) you want to quantize.

Step 3: Access the quantize function.
On most sequencers the quantize function is selected from a list of track edit options.

Step 4: Select the desired track and measure(s) to be quantized.
On most sequencers you must specify the track, the starting measure, and the ending measure.

Step 5: Select the desired resolution.
In general, you should use a quantization value equal to the shortest note value in the measure (or measures) to be quantized. For example, a measure containing sixteenth notes should be quantized to the nearest sixteenth note.

Step 6: Select the quantization percentage.

> *Note: If your sequencer does not have an option for quantization percentage or quantization amount, skip this step.*

Some sequencers allow you to specify the percentage of quantization from 0% (no quantization) to 100% (full quantization). At 100%, the note start time will be moved to the exact note resolution you specified in Step 5. At 75%, the note start times will be moved 75% from their original start times to the note resolution selected in Step 5. Lower quantization percentages can rhythmically tighten up tracks without making the tracks sound mechanical.

Step 7: Quantize the measure(s).
This is usually accomplished by pressing a button labeled "execute".

Step 8: Listen to the correction.
Verify your edit by listening to the track.

Step 9: If you made a backup copy of the original track in Step 1, erase the backup track.
To avoid possible confusion, erase the backup track as soon as all corrections have been made.

There are two points to consider before you use quantization. First, quantization will work only if you have recorded your tracks by playing along with the sequencer's metronome. Quantizing a track which was not recorded with the metronome will produce unpredictable and, in most cases, disastrous musical results.

The second point to consider before you use quantization is that in quantizing a track, you might produce rhythms which sound unnatural or unmusical compared to unquantized parts of your music. It is important to understand that rhythmically perfect music is usually not a desired goal in music performance. Sequences with every track quantized usually become rhythmically uninteresting. Therefore, use quantization sparingly.

Chapter 9

HOW TO CORRECT DYNAMICS

There are two techniques for correcting dynamics in a track: **editing key velocity data** and **creating/editing MIDI volume data.** Let's examine these two techniques in detail.

TECHNIQUE #1: CORRECTING DYNAMICS BY EDITING KEY VELOCITY DATA

On most electronic keyboards, dynamics are controlled by key **velocity sensitivity.** Velocity sensitive keyboards are usually used to control a sound's loudness and tone quality by striking the keys at various speeds. Striking a key quickly will usually make a sound louder and brighter in tone quality. Striking a key slowly will usually make a sound softer and darker in tone quality.

There are three options for correcting dynamics produced by velocity sensitivity in a sequence track - **re-recording, punch-in,** and **event editing.** Let's examine each of these options in detail.

> *Note: If your keyboard is not velocity sensitive, or if you are using a sound on your synthesizer which is not velocity sensitive, go to Technique #2 (**Correcting Dynamics Using MIDI Volume**) on p.125*

Option #1: Correcting Velocity Sensitive Dynamics By Re-Recording

If a track contains many mistakes, it's sometimes easier to erase the track and to record the part again. If you continue to make the same mistakes in the same places, you should either record the part at a slower tempo or practice the troublesome passages before continuing to record.

Option #2: Correcting Velocity Sensitive Dynamics Using Punch-In

For many performers, punch-in is usually the fastest and easiest way to correct or to improve the dynamics of a musical part. To correct velocity sensitive dynamics by using punch-in, follow the steps listed below.

Step 1: Make a backup copy of the original track.

Note: If your sequencer has an "Undo" function, skip this step.

Use the sequencer feature called "Track Copy" to make a backup copy of the original track. If you accidentally damage or erase the original track, you can use the backup copy.

Step 2: Identify the measure or measures that you want to re-record.
The starting point of the measure or notes that you want to re-record is called the **punch-in point.** The ending point is called the **punch-out point.** All of the music between these two points will be erased when you use punch-in.

Note: All sequencers do not have the same punch-in and punch-out capabilities. Some sequencers allow you to specify punch-in points and punch-out points at any location within a measure. Other sequencers allow you to specify punch-in points and punch-out points only at the beginning or at the end of a measure. If your sequencer uses only measure numbers for punch-in and punch-out points, check to see how your sequencer defines the punch-out point. On some sequencers, selecting a punch-out point at Measure 7 means that the sequencer will actually stop re-recording at the end of Measure 6. On other sequencers, a punch-out point at Measure 7 means that the sequencer will re-record through Measure 7 and will stop re-recording just before the beginning of Measure 8. Be sure you know which way your sequencer operates or you might accidentally erase one measure too many.

Step 3: Set the number of lead-in measures.
The lead-in measure number determines how many measures of the sequence you will hear before the punch-in begins. Be sure to select a lead-in point that gives you enough time to prepare for the punch-in.

Step 4: If you used a metronome when you originally recorded a track, activate the metronome before you record the punch-in.

Using the metronome will help in making your punch-in sound more consistent with the original recording and less likely to be detected.

Step 5: Be sure to select the correct track before you begin recording.

This step is very important when you are working with multi-track sequences. Be sure you have selected the track which contains the mistake in dynamics.

Step 6: Record the punch-in.

The following recording procedures will help you produce a good punch-in.

Recording Procedure #1: When recording the punch-in, start playing along with the music before the punch-in point, and continue to play after the punch-out point.

One of the audible signs of a punch-in is a sudden change in the phrasing of a musical line. Playing the part a little before the punch-in point and a little after the punch-out point will often make the punch-in less obvious by maintaining the flow of the entire musical line.

Recording Procedure #2: Match the dynamics of the punch-in music with the rest of the musical line.

Another audible sign of a punch-in is a sudden change in dynamics in the middle of a musical phrase. Be sure to match the dynamic level of the new musical material with the rest of the phrase.

Recording Procedure #3: For difficult music, slow down the song tempo to record the punch-in.

Remember, a change in the song tempo will not affect pitch. You can record the punch-in music at a slow tempo, and then have the sequencer play back the music at a faster tempo.

After you have recorded your punch-in, listen to the entire phrase very carefully. A good punch-in is inaudible. If your punch-in doesn't sound right, try to analyze what is wrong. Remember, the obvious signs of a punch-in are sudden differences in dynamics or phrasing. Once you have identified the problem, try to correct the error by punching in again.

Step 7: Insert missing notes if they occur.
Review Step 7 on p.90, if necessary.

Step 8: If you made a backup copy of the original track in Step 1, erase the backup track.
To avoid possible confusion, erase the backup track as soon as all corrections have been made.

Option #3: Correcting Velocity Sensitive Dynamics Using Event Editing

In Part 1 of this section, you will learn how note velocities are represented in the MIDI event list. In Part 2, you will learn how to use event editing to change note velocities.

PART 1 - READING NOTE VELOCITIES IN A MIDI EVENT CHART

Suppose that you record the following melody into Track 1 of your sequencer, and you use a sound that responds to velocity sensitivity.

Fig. 9.1

During the recording, however, you play (E), the first note in Measure 2 too loudly. When you play back your sequence track, the note dynamics sound like this. (See *Fig. 9.2.*)

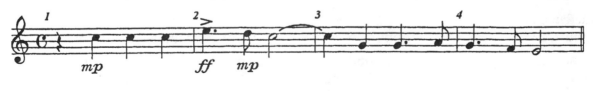

Fig. 9.2

The MIDI event list in *Fig. 9.3* represents a quantized recording of the music in *Fig. 9.2*. For the purpose of clarity, the note start times and durations are exact.

A Measure#	B Event #	C Event Type	D Start time	E Duration	F Velocity
1	1	4	2:00	0:95	72
1	2	4	3:00	0:95	70
1	3	4	4:00	0:95	69
2	1	E4	1:00	1:47	120
2	2	D4	2:48	0:47	72
2	3	C4	3:00	TIE	73
3	1	C4	TIE	0:95	---
3	2	G3	2:00	0:95	74
3	3	G3	3:00	1:47	76
3	4	A3	4:48	0:47	70
4	1	G3	1:00	1:47	73
4	2	F3	2:48	0:47	65
4	3	E3	3:00	1:95	61

Fig. 9.3

You've already learned that in *Fig. 9.3,* **Column A** lists the measures of the song; **Column B** lists the event number in each measure; and **Column C** lists the type of event. **Column D** lists the starting time for each event, and **Column E** lists the event duration. **Column F** lists the velocity level for each note. In musical terms, **Column F** represents the dynamic level for each note in the melody. By changing the values in **Column F**, you can change the dynamic level of any note.

Before you can make any changes or corrections, however, you must first understand what the numbers in **Column F** represent. You know that **Column F** lists each note's key velocity - the speed in which each key is struck. On most velocity sensitive MIDI instruments, the range of velocity values is from 0 to 127. (Some instruments might use the numbers 1 to 128.) A velocity level of 0 is silence. A velocity level of 127 is the loudest and brightest sound possible. See *Fig. 9.4*.

Velocity level	0-------16 ------32-------48-----62----78-----94-----110 ----- 127
Musical dynamic range	*ppp* *pp* *p* *mp* *mf* *f* *ff* *fff*

Fig. 9.4

PART 2 - USING EVENT EDITING TO CORRECT NOTE VELOCITIES

If you look at the list of velocity levels under **Column F** in *Fig. 9.3,* you can see that most note velocity levels fall between values of 61 and 76. It's easy to spot the note that was played too loudly. E4, the first event of Measure 2, has a velocity level of 120. To correct this mistake in dynamics using event editing, follow the steps listed below.

Step 1: Make a backup copy of the original track.

> *Note: If your sequencer has an "Undo" function, skip this step.*

Use the sequencer feature called "Track Copy" to make a backup copy of the original track. If you accidentally damage or erase the original track, you can use the backup copy. Be sure to mute the backup track.

Step 2: Identify the track and the measure number containing the mistake.
Before you enter the event editing mode, be sure you know the measure number that contains the wrong rhythm. You can usually read the measure numbers on the sequencer display while the sequence is being played back. In this lesson, the mistake is in Measure 2 of Track 1.

Step 3: Access the MIDI event list for the track containing the mistake.
On most sequencers this is a two step process. First, find the menu prompt which reads something like "EVENT EDIT", "EVENT LISTING", or "MIDI EVENT LIST". Next, specify the sequencer track that you would like to view as an event list. In this lesson, you would specify Track 1.

Step 4: Locate the measure containing the note velocity to be edited.
On most sequencers, you would place the cursor in **Column A (Measure #)** and step through the list until you come to the number 2.

Step 5: Locate the note to be edited.
On most sequencers you would place the cursor in **Column C (Event Type)** and step through each note in the measure until you come to the desired note. In this lesson, the note is Event #1 in Measure 2 (E4).

**Step 6: Correct the dynamics of the note by changing the note's velocity
level.**

Move the cursor to **Column F (Velocity)** and highlight the velocity level of 120. On
most sequencers, you can change this value simply by typing in a new value on the
keypad. (Consult your sequencer owner's manual to learn how to edit note velocity
levels.) Lower the velocity level from 120 to 76. This level will give the note a slight
accent but will also keep it in the dynamic range of the rest of the musical phrase.

Step 7: Listen to the correction.

Be sure that the desired dynamic effect is achieved. When you play back the sequence,
the edited note should now blend dynamically with the other notes in the phrase.

**Step 8: If you made a backup copy of the original track in Step 1, erase the
backup track.**

To avoid possible confusion, erase the backup track as soon as all corrections have been
made.

As you can see, event edit makes it easy to adjust the dynamic level of any note played
with a velocity sensitive sound. It's possible to gradually increase the velocity levels of
a series of notes to create a crescendo effect. *Fig. 9.5* shows the velocity levels edited to
produce this effect.

A Measure #	B Event #	C Event Type	D Start time	E Duration	F Velocity
1	1	C4	2:00	0:95	64
1	2	C4	3:00	0:95	72
1	3	C4	4:00	0:95	80
2	1	E4	1:00	1:47	88
2	2	D4	2:48	0:47	96
2	3	C4	3:00	TIE	104
3	1	C4	TIE	0:95	---
3	2	G3	2:00	0:95	112
3	3	G3	3:00	1:47	116
3	4	A3	4:48	0:47	120
4	1	G3	1:00	1:47	124
4	2	F3	2:48	0:47	127
4	3	E3	3:00	1:95	127

Fig. 9.5 Velocity levels edited to produce a crescendo effect.

It's also possible to gradually decrease the velocity levels of a series of notes to create a decrescendo effect. *Fig. 9.6* shows the velocity levels edited to produce this effect.

A Measure #	B Event #	C Event Type	D Start time	E Duration	F Velocity
1	1	C4	2:00	0:95	127
1	2	C4	3:00	0:95	120
1	3	C4	4:00	0:95	112
2	1	E4	1:00	1:47	104
2	2	D4	2:48	0:47	96
2	3	C4	3:00	TIE	88
3	1	C4	TIE	0:95	---
3	2	G3	2:00	0:95	80
3	3	G3	3:00	1:47	72
3	4	A3	4:48	0:47	70
4	1	G3	1:00	1:47	64
4	2	F3	2:48	0:47	58
4	3	E3	3:00	1:95	50

Fig. 9.6 Velocity levels edited to produce a decrescendo effect.

A few sequencers include a special feature that makes it easy to create a gradual change in note velocities over a number of measures. This feature is usually called "MODIFY VELOCITY" or "CREATE VELOCITY CURVE". When you select the "MODIFY VELOCITY" or "CREATE VELOCITY CURVE" function, the sequencer looks for the following information:

Starting Measure # _____, Starting Time_____, Starting Velocity Level_____,

Ending Measure #_____, Ending Time_____, Ending Velocity Level_____,

To create the decrescendo effect listed in *Fig. 9.6*, the screen should look like this:

Starting Measure #001, Starting Time 2:00, Starting Velocity Level 127,

Ending Measure #004, Ending Time 3:00, Ending Velocity Level 50.

After you enter this information, the sequencer will generate a smooth decrescendo effect between these two points in the music.

Note: It is important for you to remember that the editing procedure described above will work only if your instrument uses velocity sensitivity to control the sound's loudness and brightness. If a program on your instrument does not use velocity sensitivity to control the sound's loudness and brightness, you must use MIDI volume to create a crescendo or decrescendo effect. See Method #4 on p. 131.

TECHNIQUE #2: CORRECTING DYNAMICS USING MIDI VOLUME

Different types of MIDI controllers have been assigned identifying numbers. **Controller #7** in the MIDI specification is always used to control an instrument's volume level. Controller #7 has a volume level range from 0 (no output) to 127 (maximum output). In the following pages the terms "MIDI Volume" and "Controller #7" are synonymous.

It is important for you to understand the difference between controlling dynamics through velocity data and controlling dynamics through MIDI volume. When you lower the values of note velocities, in most cases you are lowering the volume level as well as making the tone quality darker. When you lower the MIDI volume, you are lowering only the volume level. This difference can be compared to a trumpet player who plays a melody very softly during a recording session, as opposed to a recording engineer who lowers the volume of a trumpet part after it has been recorded. When the trumpet player plays softly, the lower harmonics of the sound dominate, producing a darker tone quality. When the trumpet player plays loudly, the upper harmonics dominate, producing a brighter tone quality. Therefore, if the volume level of the recorded trumpet melody is lowered, the notes will be softer but the tone quality will not change. For this reason, the editing of dynamics through velocity values is usually used to control the dynamics of individual notes in a track; the editing of dynamics through MIDI volume is usually used to adjust the balance of one sequencer track with other tracks.

MIDI volume can be used to create an **instantaneous volume change** or a **gradual volume change** in a track. Let's learn how to create these two effects.

Option #1: Using MIDI Volume To Create An Instantaneous Volume Change

Look at the dynamic marking in *Fig. 9.7*.

Fig. 9.7

Now suppose that you want to create the dynamic effect shown in *Fig. 9.8*.

Fig. 9.8

This effect can be produced by inserting a MIDI volume level into the event list of the music. To create this effect using MIDI volume, follow the steps listed below.

Step 1: Make a backup copy of the original track.

Note: If your sequencer has an "Undo" function, skip this step.

Use the sequencer feature called "Track Copy" to make a backup copy of the original track. If you accidentally damage or erase the original track, you can use the backup copy. Be sure to mute the backup track.

Step 2: Identify the track and the measure in the track where you want to insert the volume change event.

Before you enter the event editing mode, be sure you know the measure number where you want to insert the volume change event. You can usually read the measure numbers on the sequencer display while the sequence is being played back. In this lesson, you want to insert the volume level on or just before Event #2 in Measure 3.

Step 3: Access the MIDI event list on your sequencer.

On most sequencers this is a two step process. First, find the menu prompt which reads something like "EVENT EDIT", "EVENT LISTING", or "MIDI EVENT LIST". Next, specify the sequencer track you would like to view as an event list.

Step 4: Locate the measure in the track where you want to insert the volume change event.

On most sequencers you would place the cursor in the "Measure#" column and step through the measures by pressing the "+" button or "value up" key. In this lesson, you want to insert the volume change command on or just before the second beat of Measure 3.

Step 5: Insert the volume change event into the MIDI event list.

On some sequencers, you can insert volume change events into an event list by selecting "MIDI Volume" or "Controller #7" from a list of several types of MIDI events. After you make your selection, press the *enter* key or the *insert* key on the sequencer keypad to add the new event into the measure. (Consult your sequencer owner's manual to learn how to insert events into a measure.)

On other sequencers, you can insert a volume change event into an event list by copying an existing adjacent event and then changing the copied event into a volume change command. For example, to insert a volume change on beat 2 of Measure 3 in *Fig. 9.9*, you must first duplicate or copy another event in Measure 3. You can copy any event in the measure. For this example, copy Event #2 - the note G3. On most sequencers, you can copy an event by placing the cursor on the event to be copied and selecting "event copy", "duplicate", or "insert" from a list of editing options.

A	B	C	D	E	F
Measure #	Event #	Event Type	Start time	Duration	Velocity
1	1	C4	2:00	0:95	127
1	2	C4	3:00	0:95	120
1	3	C4	4:00	0:95	112
2	1	E4	1:00	1:47	104
2	2	D4	2:48	0:47	96
2	3	C4	3:00	TIE	88
3	1	C4	TIE	0:95	---
3	2	G3	2:00	0:95	80
3	3	G3	2:00	0:95	80
3	4	G3	3:00	1:47	72
3	5	A3	4:48	0:47	70
4	1	G3	1:00	1:47	64
4	2	F3	2:48	0:47	58
4	3	E3	3:00	1:95	50

Fig. 9.9 In Measure 3, Event #3 is a copy of Event #2.

After an event has been copied, you must change the copied event into a volume change command. This is usually done by placing the cursor under **Column C (Event Type)** of the copied event and changing the event type to the abbreviation "CNTRL 7" (for controller 7), or "VOL" (for MIDI Volume) from a list of MIDI event types. (Consult your owner's manual to learn how to copy events and how to change event types.) See *Fig. 9.10.*

A Measure #	B Event #	C Event Type	D Start time	E Duration	F Velocity
1	1	C4	2:00	0:95	127
1	2	C4	3:00	0:95	120
1	3	C4	4:00	0:95	112
2	1	E4	1:00	1:47	104
2	2	D4	2:48	0:47	96
2	3	C4	3:00	TIE	88
3	1	C4	TIE	0:95	-
3	2	G3	2:00	0:95	80
3	3	CNTRL 7	2:00	--	127
3	4	G3	3:00	1:47	72
3	5	A3	4:48	0:47	70
4	1	G3	1:00	1:47	64
4	2	F3	2:48	0:47	58
4	3	E3	3:00	1:95	50

Fig. 9.10 Create a volume change event by changing the **EVENT TYPE** *from G3 to* **CNTRL 7** *(or* **VOL***).*

Notice that when the event type is changed from a note to a volume change command, the value in the duration disappears. Volume change commands are single events with a duration of only one clock pulse. On some sequencers the value "127" will appear under **Column F** (Velocity). This might be confusing, because it appears as if Controller #7 has a velocity value. The "127" in this case represents the volume level of the volume change event. See Step 6.

Step 6: Enter the desired volume level.
Move the cursor under **Column F**. Remember, when the event type is MIDI volume, **Column F** represents "volume level", not "note velocity". Adjust the value from 127 to 50.

Step 7: Enter the desired start time for the volume change event.

When you copied Event #2 in Measure 3, you copied all of the values for that event. Therefore, the start time for the volume change event should already be set to 2:00. If it isn't set to 2:00 on your sequencer, move the cursor under **Column D** and change the start time to 2:00.

Step 8: Listen to the correction.

Listen to the track. If the volume change in Measure 3 is not satisfactory, go back into the event list and edit the value for the volume change event.

Step 9: If you made a backup copy of the original track in Step 1, erase the backup track.

To avoid possible confusion, erase the backup track as soon as all corrections have been made.

Option #2: Using MIDI Volume To Create A Gradual Volume Change

Suppose you want to create the decrescendo effect shown in *Fig. 9.11*.

Fig. 9.11

There are four methods for creating gradual change in dynamics using MIDI volume:

1. **Recording The Volume Changes On A Separate Track.**
2. **Overdubbing The Volume Changes On A Track Which Already Contains Music.**
3. **Recording The Volume Changes While You Record The Music.**
4. **Using The Sequencer's Crescendo/Decrescendo Feature.**

Let's examine each of these methods in detail.

Method #1: Recording The Volume Changes While You Record The Music.
In some cases, it might be possible to record the volume changes while you record the music. Most keyboards have control inputs for volume pedals. In many cases, the volume pedal changes can be recorded into a sequencer as MIDI volume data. To create the decrescendo effect in *Fig. 9.11,* start recording the music with the volume pedal all the way down, and then gradually use your heel on the pedal to lower the volume while you are playing. The sequencer will simultaneously record the MIDI data generated by the keyboard as well as the MIDI controller data generated by the volume pedal.

Note: On some sequencers, it may be necessary to insert the desired starting volume level as the first event of the track. Adding this event ensures that the track will begin at the desired volume. If this step is necessary, refer to Option #1 on p. 126.

Method #2: Overdubbing The Volume Changes On A Track Which Already Contains Music.

Note: If your sequencer does not have an overdub mode, go to Method #3.

Overdubbing means to record new information on a track without erasing any information already on the track. For example, on Track 1 of a sequencer you might record the right hand part of a piano piece. If your sequencer has an overdub recording mode, you could then record the left hand part on Track 1 without erasing the right hand part already recorded.

If your sequencer has an overdub mode, it might be possible for you to record the music and then, during playback, overdub the volume changes. This technique is useful when you want to add volume changes to a specific track after you have recorded several other tracks.

Method #3 - Recording The Volume Changes On A Separate Track.
This method is functionally identical to Method #2. The only difference is that you record the volume change commands on another sequencer track, rather than overdub them on the track that contains the music. Suppose that your music is recorded on Track 1 and suppose that Track 1 is set to MIDI Channel 1. To record the volume changes on Track 2, first assign Track 2's MIDI channel to channel 1. Next, put Track

2 into record mode. When you start recording, you will hear the notes played on Track 1. The foot pedal data will be recorded on Track 2. Because Track 2 is set to the same MIDI channel as Track 1, you will hear the volume level of the music change as you move the foot pedal.

On most sequencers you can merge the data on Track 2 with Track 1 by using a function called **track merging** or **track bouncing**. This function is useful if you think you might not have enough tracks for your sequence. (Consult your manual to learn about merging or bouncing tracks.) If you don't need the track, however, there is no reason to merge the tracks. Leave the volume data on Track 2 and name the track "Track 1 Volume".

> *Note: On some sequencers, it may be necessary to insert the desired starting volume level as the first event of the track. Adding this event ensures that the track will begin at the desired volume. If this step is necessary, refer to Option #1 on p. 126.*

Method #4: Using The Sequencer's Crescendo/Decrescendo Feature.

> *Note: This feature is not available on all sequencers.*

A few sequencers make it easy to create a gradual change in dynamics over a number of measures. This feature is usually called "MODIFY VOLUME", "CREATE VOLUME CURVE", or "CREATE VOLUME CRESCENDO/DECRESCENDO". When you select this feature, the sequencer looks for the following information:

Starting Measure # _____, Starting Time_____, Starting Volume Level_____,
Ending Measure # _____, Ending Time_____, Ending Volume Level_____,

To create the decrescendo effect listed in *Fig. 9.11,* the screen should look like this:

Starting Measure #001, Starting Time 1:00, Starting Volume Level 127,
Ending Measure #004, Ending Time 4:00, Ending Volume Level 40.

After you enter this information, the sequencer will generate a smooth decrescendo effect between these two points in the music.

Chapter 10

HOW TO CHANGE SYNTHESIZER SOUNDS (PROGRAMS)

In this chapter you will learn how to change synthesizer sounds or **programs.** The word **program** means a specific sound in a synthesizer's memory. For example, Program #3 might be a piano sound, Program #21 might be a bass guitar, and so on. Many of today's instruments can easily store 100 or 200 different programs.

Before you learn how to change programs in a track, be sure that you understand how sequencers work with MIDI **program change commands.** A MIDI program change command is an event that tells a MIDI instrument to select or to call up a specific program. When you select a program on your keyboard, a MIDI program change command is automatically generated. MIDI program numbers range from 0 to 127, with 0 as the first program on a synthesizer.

In Chapter 3, you learned how to select the starting program number for a track. The program number that you select will be used throughout the track unless you create a program change command in the track. There are four techniques for creating program changes in a sequencer track:

1. **Recording The Program Changes While You Record The Music.**
2. **Overdubbing The Program Changes On A Track Which Already Contains Music.**
3. **Recording The Program Changes On A Separate Track.**
4. **Inserting The Program Changes Into A Recorded Track Using Event Edit.**

Let's examine each of these techniques in detail.

Technique #1: Recording The Program Changes While You Record The Music.

In some cases, it might be possible to record the program changes while you record the music. For example, let's suppose you want to record the following music into a sequencer.

Fig. 10.1

Instead of using one sound for the entire phrase, however, let's suppose that you want to use a guitar sound in Measure 1, a vocal sound in Measure 2, and a piano sound in Measures 3 and 4. See *Fig. 10.2*.

Fig. 10.2

Now let's suppose that, on your synthesizer, the guitar sound is Program #23, the vocal sound is Program #11, and the piano sound is Program #42. If you play the music at a very slow tempo, you might be able to enter the two digits for each successive program during the last beat of Measures 1 and 2. If, however, you were playing either at a fast tempo or with both hands on the keyboard, you would not have enough time to change programs manually.

You can solve this problem by changing programs with a foot switch. Most electronic instruments provide an input jack for a **program advance foot switch.** This type of foot switch enables you to advance programs in consecutive order. For example, suppose that your instrument is set to Program #23. When you step on the program advance foot switch, the instrument will advance to Program #24, which is the next consecutive program number. If you step on the foot switch again, the instrument will advance to Program #25.

When you use a foot switch to change programs, you can keep both hands on the keyboard. However, all of the program changes for your music must be in put sequential order. On most electronic keyboards, there is no way to use a program advance foot switch to step from Program #23 to any program other than #24. Therefore, if you want to use a program advance foot switch, you must copy the sounds to different program locations so that the programs are in the correct sequential order for the music.

For example, in *Fig. 10.2*, you want to hear the guitar sound (Program #23) in Measure 1, the vocal sound (Program #11) in Measure 2, and the piano sound (Program #42) in Measures 3 and 4. In order to select these sounds with a foot switch, you would have to copy Program #11 to Program #24, and then copy Program #42 to Program #25. Your program list would be as follows:

Program #23 (guitar)
Program #24 (vocal)
Program #25 (piano)

Now you can record everything at one time - the music with your hands on the keyboard, and the program changes with one foot on the program advance foot switch.

Before you consult your synthesizer manual to learn how to copy programs, read the remainder of this chapter to learn other techniques for recording program changes. If you then decide to use this technique, follow your manual's instructions carefully , or else you might permanently erase some of your sounds.

Technique #2: Overdubbing The Program Changes On A Track Which Already Contains Music.

Note: If your sequencer does not have an overdub mode, go to Technique #3.

Overdubbing means to record new information on a track without erasing any information already on the track. For example, on Track 1 of a sequencer you might record the right hand part of a piano piece. If your sequencer has an overdub recording mode, you could then record the left hand part on Track 1 without erasing the right hand part already recorded.

If your sequencer has an overdub mode, it might be possible for you to record the music and then, during playback, overdub the program changes. However, it is usually much easier to insert program change commands by using EVENT EDIT - the method described in Technique #4.

Technique #3: Recording The Program Changes On A Separate Track.

This technique is functionally identical to Technique #2. The only difference is that you record the program change commands on another sequencer track rather than overdub them on the track that contains the music. Let's suppose that your music is recorded on Track 1 and that Track 1 is set to MIDI channel 1. To add program changes on Track 2, begin by assigning Track 2's MIDI channel to channel 1. Next, put Track 2 into record mode. When you start recording, you will hear the notes played on Track 1. Your program changes will be recorded on Track 2. Because Track 2 and Track 1 are set to the same MIDI channel, you will hear the sounds change as you select different program numbers.

On most sequencers you can merge the data on Track 2 with Track 1 by using a function called **track merging** or **track bouncing**. This function is useful if you think you might not have enough tracks for your sequence. (Consult your manual to learn about merging or bouncing tracks.) If you don't need the track, however, there is no reason to merge the tracks. Leave the program change data on Track 2 and name the track "Track 1 Program Changes".

Technique #4: Inserting Program Change Commands Into A Recorded Track Using Event Edit.

Fig. 10.3 is a MIDI event list of the music in *Fig. 10.2*.

Measure #1	Event #	Event Type	Start time	Duration	Velocity
1	1	D3	1:00	1:47	92
1	2	E3	2:48	0:47	83
1	3	F#3	3:00	0:95	81
2	1	G3	1:00	1:47	94
2	2	A3	2:48	0:47	84
2	3	B3	3:00	0:95	82
3	1	C#4	1:00	1:47	90
3	2	D4	2:48	0:47	79
3	3	E4	3:00	0:95	88
3	4	D4	4:00	0:47	84
3	5	C#4	4:48	0:47	80
4	1	D4	1:00	2:95	89

Fig. 10.3 The MIDI event list for the music in Fig. 10.2.

In order to add program change commands to this event list, you must *insert* the program change commands as new events in the list. This can be accomplished in the following steps:

Step 1:   Make a backup copy of the original track.

Note: If your sequencer has an "Undo" function, skip this step.

Use a sequencer feature called "Track Copy" to make a backup copy of the original track. If you accidentally damage or erase the original track, you can use the backup copy. Be sure to mute the backup track.

Step 2:   Identify the track and measure number where you want to insert the program change command.

Before you enter the event editing mode, be sure you know the track and measure number where you want to insert the program change command. In this lesson, you want to insert program change commands in Measures 1 and 2.

Step 3:   Access the MIDI event list for the track.

On most sequencers this is a two step process. First, find the menu prompt which reads something like "EVENT EDIT", "EVENT LISTING", or "MIDI EVENT LIST". Next, specify the sequencer track you would like to view as an event list. In this lesson you want to view Track 1.

Step 4:   Locate the measure in the track where you want to insert the program change command.

On most sequencers you would place the cursor in the "Measure #" column and step through each note in the measure until you come to the desired note. In Fig. *10.3*, the first program change command will be inserted at the end of Measure 1.

Step 5:   Insert the program change event into the MIDI event list.

On some sequencers, you can insert program change events into an event list by selecting the phrase "program change" or "PROG" from a list of several types of MIDI events. After you select "program change", you press the *enter* key or the *insert* key on the sequencer keypad to add the new event into the measure. (Consult your sequencer owner's manual to learn how to insert events into a measure.)

On other sequencers, you can insert a program change command into an event list by copying an existing event and then changing the copied event into a program change command. For example, to insert a program change on the last beat of Measure 1 in *Fig. 10.3*, you must first duplicate or copy another event in Measure 1. You can copy any event in the measure. For this example, copy Event #3 - the note F#3. On most sequencers, you copy an event by placing the cursor on the event to be copied and selecting "event copy", "duplicate", or "insert" from a list of editing options. See *Fig. 10.4*.

Measure #	Event #	Event Type	Start time	Duration	Velocity
1	1	D3	1:00	1:47	92
1	2	E3	2:48	0:47	83
1	3	F#3	3:00	0:95	81
1	4	F#3	3:00	0:95	81

Fig. 10.4. Event #4 is a copy of Event #3.

After an event has been copied, you must change the copied event into a program change command. This is usually done by placing the cursor under **Event Type** and selecting the abbreviation PROG (for program). See *Fig. 10.5*. (Consult your owner's manual to learn how to copy events and how to change event types.)

Measure #	Event #	Event Type	Start time	Duration	Velocity
1	1	D3	1:00	1:47	92
1	2	E3	2:48	0:47	83
1	3	F#4	3:00	0:95	81
1	4	PROG---	3:00	------	---

*Fig. 10.5. Create a program change command by changing the **EVENT TYPE** for F#4 to **PROG**.*

Notice that when the event type is changed from a note to a program change command, the values in the duration and velocity columns disappear. Program change commands are single events with a duration of only one clock pulse and with no velocity level.

Step 6: Enter the desired program number.
In this example, you want to hear the vocal sound (Program #11) in Measure 2. Enter the number 11 after the PROG abbreviation. You can do this by placing the cursor after the PROG abbreviation and typing the desired program number. See *Fig. 10.6*. (Consult your owner's manual to learn how to enter program numbers in event edit.)

Measure #	Event #	Event Type	Start time	Duration	Velocity
1	1	D3	1:00	1:47	92
1	2	E3	2:48	0:47	83
1	3	F#3	3:00	0:95	81
1	4	PROG 11	3:00	------	---

Fig. 10.6. Add the desired program number to the **Event Type** *column.*

Step 7: Enter the desired start time in the measure where the program change should occur.

It's a good idea to avoid changing programs while sustaining notes. Many electronic instruments will terminate a note as soon as a program change command is received. In *Fig. 10.3*, the last note in Measure 1 (F#3) starts on the third beat and is held until the beginning of the fourth beat. This means that the program change command can occur anytime after the first clock pulse of the fourth beat. It is usually desirable to put a program change command just before the first note of the new sound. If you again look at *Fig. 10.3*, you can see that the next note event is G3, which starts on the first beat of Measure 2. Put the program change command start time in Measure 1 at 4:90. This start time is 6 clock pulses before the G3 in Measure 2. On most sequencers, an event's start time can be changed by placing the cursor on the existing start time and then typing in the new time. See Fig. 10.7. (Consult your owner's manual to learn how to change an event's start time.)

Measure #	Event #	Event Type	Start time	Duration	Velocity
1	1	D3	1:00	1:47	92
1	2	E3	2:48	0:47	83
1	3	F#3	3:00	0:95	81
1	4	PROG 11	4:90	------	---

Fig. 10.7 Select the start time for the program change command.

Repeat Steps 2-8 and insert a program change command for Program 42 at the end of Measure 2.

Step 8: Listen to the track.

Step 9: If you made a backup copy of the original track in Step 1, erase the backup track.

To avoid possible confusion, erase the backup track as soon as all corrections have been made.

Chapter 11

HOW TO CHANGE TEMPO IN A SEQUENCE

Tempo is the performance speed of a musical composition. A tempo mark is an indication of the desired speed of performance. At one point in history, classical composers used generalized terms such as *adagio* (slow) or *allegro ma non troppo* (fast but not too fast) to indicate the tempo of music. Today, however, most composers indicate tempo by using a precise measurement of time called the **bpm** marking (*beats per minute*). *Bpm* tempo markings are usually displayed as "120 *bpm*", or just "120". This means that the tempo is equal to 120 quarter notes played in one minute. Higher *bpm* values indicate faster tempos. For example, a song with a tempo marking of 180 *bpm* should be played twice as fast as a song with a tempo marking of 90 *bpm*. Most sequencers use *bpm* values to display a song's tempo. You can change a song's tempo on most sequencers by placing the cursor on the tempo indicator and typing the desired *bpm* value.

There are two types of tempo changes possible in a song - **instantaneous tempo changes** and **gradual tempo changes**. Let's examine the techniques for adding each type of tempo change to a sequence.

TECHNIQUE #1: CREATING INSTANTANEOUS TEMPO CHANGES

There are two options for creating instantaneous changes in tempo: **using a dedicated tempo track,** and **using event editing** Let's examine these techniques in detail.

Option #1: Using A Dedicated Tempo Track.

Note: If your sequencer does not have a dedicated tempo track, see Technique #2.

Suppose that you record the music in *Fig. 11.1* into a sequencer at a tempo of 100 *bpm*.

Fig. 11.1

Let's suppose that you want to make some extreme tempo changes in the music. You decide to change the tempo to 200 *bpm* in Measure 2 and to 50 *bpm* in Measure 3. See *Fig. 11.2*.

Fig. 11.2

To create the tempo changes as specified in *Fig. 11.2*, perform the following steps:

Step 1: Identify the locations in the music where you want to insert a tempo change command.

In this lesson, you want to insert the first tempo change command at the beginning of Measure 2.

Step 2: Access the tempo track on your sequencer.

(Consult your sequencer manual to learn how to access the tempo track.)

Step 3: Locate the measure in the tempo track where you want to insert the first tempo change.

In Fig. *11.2*, the first tempo change will occur in Measure 2.

Step 4: Insert the tempo change command into the tempo track.

In most cases, you insert tempo change commands into the tempo track by pressing the *insert* key on the sequencer keypad. (Consult your manual to learn how to enter tempo change commands into a tempo track.)

Step 5: Enter the desired tempo.

This is usually done by pressing the *insert* key on the keypad and then typing in the desired *bpm* value. In this example, the *bpm* value is 200. (Consult your manual to learn how to enter *bpm* values in a tempo track.)

Step 6: Enter the desired start time for the tempo change command.

Some sequencers allow tempo change commands only on the first beat of a measure. Other sequencers allow tempo change commands at any location in a measure. For this example, enter the tempo change exactly on 1:00, the first beat of Measure 2.

Step 7: Listen to the music.

You should hear Measure 1 at a tempo of 100 *bpm*, and Measures 2-4 at a tempo of 200 *bpm*. When you insert a tempo change command in the tempo track, the new tempo will remain in effect until you insert another tempo change command. Repeat steps 1-7 to insert the tempo change command of 50 *bpm* at the beginning of Measure 3.

Option #2: Using Event Edit

If your sequencer doesn't have a separate tempo track, you can insert a tempo change command into a track by using event editing. *Fig. 11.3* is the MIDI event list for the music in *Fig. 11.2*.

Measure #1	Event #	Event Type	Start time	Duration	Velocity
1	1	D3	1:00	1:47	92
1	2	E3	2:48	0:47	83
1	3	F#3	3:00	0:95	81
2	1	G3	1:00	1:47	94
2	2	A3	2:48	0:47	84
2	3	B3	3:00	0:95	82
3	1	C#4	1:00	1:47	90
3	2	D4	2:48	0:47	79
3	3	E4	3:00	0:95	88
3	4	D4	4:00	0:47	84
3	5	C#4	4:48	0:47	80
4	1	D4	1:00	2:95	89

Fig. 11.3. The MIDI event list for the music in Fig. 11.2.

In order to add tempo change commands to the event list in *Fig. 11.3*, you must insert the tempo change commands as new events in the list. You can accomplish this by performing the following steps:

Step 1: Make a backup copy of the original track.
Use the sequencer feature called "Track Copy" to make a backup copy of the original track. If you accidentally damage or erase the original track, you can use backup copy. Be sure to mute the backup track.

Step 2: Identify the track and the measure in the track where you want to insert the tempo change command.
Before you enter the event editing mode, be sure you know the track number and the measure number where you want to insert a tempo change command. In this lesson, you want to insert the first tempo change command at the beginning of Measure 2.

Step 3: Access the MIDI event list for the desired track.
On most sequencers this is a two step process. First, find the menu prompt which reads something like "EVENT EDIT", "EVENT LISTING", or "MIDI EVENT LIST". Next, specify the sequencer track you would like to view as an event list. In this lesson, you would view Track 1.

Step 4: - Locate the measure in the track where you want to insert the tempo change command.
On most sequencers you would place the cursor in the "Measure #" column and step through each note in the measure until you come to the desired note. Be sure the MIDI event list is displaying the measure where you want to insert the tempo change command. In *Fig. 11.3*, the first tempo change command will be inserted at the beginning of Measure 2.

Step 5: Insert the tempo change event into the MIDI event list.
On some sequencers, you can insert tempo change events into an event list by selecting the phrase "tempo change" or "TEMP" from a list of several types of MIDI events. After you select "tempo change", press the *enter* key or the *insert* key on the sequencer keypad to add the new event into the measure. (Consult your sequencer owner's manual to learn how to insert tempo change events into a measure.)

On other sequencers, you can insert tempo change events into an event list by copying an existing event in the measure and then changing the copied event into a tempo change command. For example, to insert a tempo change on the first beat of Measure 2 in *Fig. 11.2*, you must duplicate or copy the first event in Measure 2. See *Fig. 11.4*.

Measure #	Event #	Event Type	Start time	Duration	Velocity
2	1	G3	1:00	1:47	92
2	2	G3	1:00	1:47	92
2	3	A3	2:48	0:47	84
2	4	B3	3:00	0:95	82

Fig. 11.4. Event #2 is a copy of Event #1.

After an event has been copied, you must change the copied event into a tempo change command. You can do this by moving the cursor to the Event Type column and then typing the abbreviation TEMP (for tempo). You can also select the tempo change command from a list of MIDI event types. See *Fig. 11.5*. (Consult your owner's manual to learn how to copy events and how to change event types.)

Measure #	Event #	Event Type	Start time	Duration	Velocity
2	1	G3	1:00	1:47	92
2	2	TEMP---	1:00	----	---
2	3	A3	2:48	0:47	84
2	4	B3	3:00	0:95	82

Fig. 11.5. Create a tempo change command by changing the
Event Type *for G3 to* **TEMP**.

Notice that when the event type is changed from a note to a tempo change command, the values in the duration and velocity columns disappear. Tempo change commands are single events with a duration of only one clock pulse and with no velocity level.

Step 6: Enter the desired tempo.
In this example, you want the tempo to be 200 *bpm* at the beginning of Measure 2. Enter the number "200" after the TEMP abbreviation by placing the cursor to the right of the TEMP abbreviation and then typing the desired tempo. See *Fig. 11.6*. (Consult your owner's manual to learn how to enter *bpm* values in event edit.)

Measure #	Event #	Event Type	Start time	Duration	Velocity
2	1	G3	1:00	1:47	92
2	2	TEMP200	1:00	----	---
2	3	A3	2:48	0:47	84
2	4	B3	3:00	0:95	82

*Fig. 11.6. Add the desired tempo to the **Event Type** column.*

Step 7: Enter the desired start time for the tempo change command

In Chapter 10, you learned that many electronic instruments cannot change programs while sustaining notes. Tempo change commands, however, do not affect the sound of an electronic instrument; they affect the speed in which the sounds are played. Therefore, tempo change commands can occur while notes are being played. *Fig. 11.5* shows two different MIDI events occurring on beat 1:00 - the sounding of the note G3, and the command to increase the tempo to 200 *bpm*. Both events are executed.

Step 8: Listen to the music.

Verify your edit by listening to the track.

Step 9: If you made a backup copy of the original track in Step 1, erase the backup track.

To avoid possible confusion, erase the backup track as soon as all corrections have been made.

TECHNIQUE #2: CREATING GRADUAL TEMPO CHANGES

There are three options for creating gradual changes in tempo:

1: Recording The Tempo Changes On The Tempo Track While The Music Is Playing Back.

2: Creating A Series Of Tempo Change Commands In The Tempo Track Or InThe MIDI Event List.

3: Using The Sequencer's Tempo Sliding Feature.

Let's examine these options in detail.

Option #1: Recording The Tempo Changes On The Tempo Track While The Music Is Playing Back.

On some sequencers you can use the plus (+) and minus (-) keys or the data slider to increase or to decrease the tempo while the music is playing. When you record on the tempo track, the sequencer will record your tempo variations instead of recording notes. This option is the easiest and fastest way to add gradual changes in tempo.

Option #2: Creating A Series Of Tempo Change Commands In Either The Tempo Track Or The MIDI Event List.

Suppose that you want a gradual decrease in tempo from 100 *bpm* to 70 *bpm* in a three measure phrase. It's possible for you to insert perhaps four or five tempo change commands into either the tempo track or the MIDI event list. Each tempo change command would be at a slightly slower tempo than the previous command, and the last command would set the tempo at 70 *bpm*. For example, the tempo changes might be as follows: 100 *bpm*, 90 *bpm*, 80 *bpm*, 70 *bpm*.

Option #2 has the following drawbacks when compared to Option #1:
- It takes time to create four or five tempo change commands and to insert them in different measures on either the tempo track or the MIDI event list.
- In order to hear the tempo changes you must leave the edit mode and return to playback mode. If one tempo change command is too fast or too slow, you must enter edit mode, find the specific tempo change command, correct the *bpm* value, and then play back the music again to hear the results.

Option #3: Using The Sequencer's Tempo Sliding Feature.

Note: Some sequencers do not have this feature.

A few sequencers make it easy for you to create gradual tempo changes over a number of measures. This feature is sometimes called **TEMPO SLIDING**. Suppose that you want a decrease in tempo from 100 *bpm* to 70 *bpm* in a three measure phrase. When you select the automatic tempo sliding feature, the sequencer will request the following information:

Starting Measure # _____ , Starting Time_____ , Starting Tempo_____*bpm*,
Ending Measure _____ , Ending Time_____ , Ending Tempo_____*bpm*.

In this lesson, the screen should look like this:

> **Starting Measure # 001, Starting Time 1:00, Starting Tempo 100** *bpm*,
> **Ending Measure #003, Ending Time 3:95, Ending Tempo 70** *bpm*

After you enter this information, the sequence will slow down gradually and evenly, so that by the end of Measure 3 the tempo will be 70 *bpm*. (Consult your manual to learn how to select the measure boundaries for a programmed tempo change.)

Small changes in tempo are one of the best ways to add expression and musicality to a sequence. A tempo change as small as two or three *bpm* can help push a phrase forward or pull it back. Experiment with all of these techniques and add whatever tempo changes you need to make your sequences more musical.

INDEX

DUPLICATE SETUP CHARTS
(Remove or photo-copy for reference)

CHAPTER 3 SETUP CHART (*FIG. 3.6*) p.33

For External
Sequencers

Sequencer Track Name	Synthesizer MIDI Channel	Synthesizer Program Name	Synthesizer Program Number	Sequencer Track Number	Sequencer Track MIDI Channel
Melody	5	Piano	23	1	5

CHAPTER 4 SETUP CHART (*FIG. 4.6*) p.44

For External
Sequencers

Sequencer Track Name	Synthesizer MIDI Channel	Synthesizer Program Name	Synthesizer Program Number	Sequencer Track Number	Sequencer Track MIDI Channel
Soprano	(5)	Pipe Organ	28	1	5
Alto	(5)	Pipe Organ	28	2	5
Tenor	(5)	Pipe Organ	28	3	5
Bass	(5)	Pipe Organ	28	4	5

CHAPTER 5 SETUP CHART (*FIG. 5.7*) p.58

For External
Sequencers

Sequencer Track Name	Synthesizer Timbre Number	Synthesizer Timbre MIDI Channel	Synthesizer Program Name	Synthesizer Program Number	Sequencer Track Number	Sequencer Track MIDI Channel
Soprano	1	(5)	Flute	24	1	5
Alto	2	(6)	Oboe	13	2	6
Tenor	3	(7)	Clarinet	47	3	7
Bass	4	(8)	Bassoon	11	4	8

CHAPTER 6 SETUP CHART (*FIG. 6.7*) p.74

Sequencer Track Name	Instrument	Instrument Function	Instrument MIDI Channel	Instrument Program Name	Instrument Program Number	Sequencer Track Number	Sequencer Track MIDI Channel
Soprano	Synthesizer A	Slave A	5	Flute	24	1	5
Alto	Synthesizer B	Slave B	6	Oboe	13	2	6
Tenor	Synthesizer C	Slave C	7	Clarinet	47	3	7
Bass	Synthesizer D	Master Keyboard	8	Bassoon	11	4	8

SETUP CHART FOR MULTI-TIMBRAL SYNTHESIZERS

(Photo-copy and use when creating your own sequences)

SEQUENCE NAME: _____

For External Sequencers

Sequencer Track Name	Synthesizer Timbre Number	Synthesizer Timbre MIDI Channel	Synthesizer Program Name	Synthesizer Program Number	Sequencer Track Number	Sequencer Track MIDI Channel

SETUP CHART FOR MONO-TIMBRAL SYNTHESIZERS

(Photo-copy and use when creating your own sequences)

SEQUENCE NAME: _____

Sequencer Track Name	Instrument	Instrument Function	Instrument MIDI Channel	Instrument Program Name	Instrument Program Number	Sequencer Track Number	Sequencer Track MIDI Channel